DEAN CUISINE
or
THE LIBERATED MAN'S GUIDE TO FINE COOKING

DEAN CUISINE

or

THE LIBERATED MAN'S GUIDE TO FINE COOKING

Jack Greenberg

and

James Vorenberg

The Sheep Meadow Press
Riverdale-on-Hudson, New York

All inquiries and permission requests should be addressed to:
    The Sheep Meadow Press
    P.O. Box 1345
    Riverdale-on-Hudson, New York 10471.

Cover design by S. M.
Photography by Deborah Greenberg
Book design and typesetting by Keystrokes, Lenox, Massachusetts
Printed by Princeton University Press

Library of Congress Cataloging-in-Publication Data:

Greenberg, Jack and Vorenberg, James
Dean Cuisine *or* The Liberated Man's Guide to Fine Cooking / Jack Greenberg and James Vorenberg
    p.   cm.
ISBN 0-935296-99-9

Printed in the United States of America

To Betty and Debby,
potscrubbers and
cheerleaders extraordinary

TABLE OF CONTENTS

DEAN CUISINE
or
THE LIBERATED MAN'S GUIDE TO FINE COOKING

CHAPTER I

Introduction

Why and How We Wrote This Book

More than ten years ago we and our wives rented a house for a month in Eze Village on the Cote d'Azur. We did almost all the marketing and cooking; our wives shopped and cooked only once in a while. Out of the experience and its discoveries we decided to write this book. But it wasn't so easy. Our jobs were demanding and over time changed. At the outset Jim was a law professor at Harvard and then Associate Dean; Jack was Director-Counsel of the NAACP Legal Defense and Educational Fund. We thought the title "The Liberated Man's Guide to Fine Cooking" described what we were trying to write. But then Jim became Dean of Harvard Law School, an impediment to completing the book quickly. At the same time, we thought, the idea of the liberated man perhaps had become too commonplace to serve as part of a catchy title. We toyed with the idea of "The Dean and Director Cookbook." As we pondered the possibility of being sued for trademark infringement by Dean and Deluca, New York's famous gourmet shop, Jack left the job as Director-Counsel and became a professor at Columbia Law School, and then Vice-Dean. The Dean and Vice Dean Cookbook didn't sound terribly euphonious nor did the zany variation: Gumbo Dean (pronounced indistinctly as Gunga Din) Cookbook, although we do have some Indian recipes.* To complicate matters, in 1989 Jack became Dean of Columbia College and Jim retired as Dean and once more became Roscoe Pound Professor of Law at Harvard. So we were about to return to "The Liberated Man's Guide to Fine Cooking," when, the Columbia Spectator, in an article

---

*Another suggestion was The Duodenal Cookbook. We rejected this as tasteless.

about a gumbo dinner which Jack cooked, called it "Dean Cuisine." The book took longer than we'd anticipated—and in the meantime we discovered new recipes and developed new tastes. Anyway, now it is done.

Our impression is that while the concept of the "liberated man" is more widely accepted than when we started and there are more of them, the demand for male liberation among women has increased exponentially. And so, we hope the book will fill a need.

Fairness requires acknowledgement that Jack supplied many more recipes than Jim. In the early stages the work was shared about equally. But as the seventies gave way to the eighties, the pressure of Jim's deanship, combined with extensive foreign travel by Jack, resulted in an imbalance. Each time Jack went off on a human rights project abroad, Jim would brace himself for another spate of foreign recipes. One of Jim's main contributions was to apply a measure of restraint—thus protecting readers from Mexican grilled grasshoppers and Philippine fertilized duck-eggs.

And when the project seemed destined to grind to a permanent halt, Betty Vorenberg provided both substantive and editing work that enabled us to finish.

Despite the uneven pace of progress on this project, there have been many high moments. For example, one day a few years ago the Dean of Harvard Law School was urgently called out of a conference by the Vice Dean of Columbia Law School, who, in a state of high excitement, reported—"I've done it—I've cracked the ceviche problem. I've brought it in under 60 minutes." (Readers can, by referring to p.17, make their own judgment of the importance of this breakthrough).

We have written out of our experiences because we enjoy good food; we enjoy preparing it and we wanted to share that pleasure with others. We believe that even the everyday meal prepared by one who returns from a full and demanding work-day need not—and should not—be ordinary. At least one part of the meal can offer a particularly delicious flavor, striking appearance, the exploratory pleasure of trying something for the first time, or simply the knowledge that the preparer has devoted enough imagination and spirit to offer something personal and special. This is not to deny the value of presenting periodically long-time family favorites, or occasionally the simplest of preparations (e.g., broiled lamb chops, boiled shrimp), but rather to suggest that with food, as else-where in our lives, what was once comfortably familiar may be-come boring. And even those members of a family who assert and believe they do not give a damn about food may develop the ability to find pleasure in special offerings, or, at least, to share the plea-sure of others.

Liberated?* The title suggests that the book is for the liber-ated man, and that raises the question: Liberated from what? To engage in serious, ambitious cooking on a frequent basis—not just as a rare showy event—involves some degree of liberation from sexual stereotypes. Just as it is difficult for some women to break with the image of mother, cook, home-maker and nothing else, some men may find the need to market and to cook a threat to their masculinity. (Stereotypes are sometimes inscrutable and die hard: the father of one of us refused to market at the grocery, under no circumstances would go to the laundry, but thought it O.K. to purchase at the butcher.) When a woman who has a work-ing life of her own lives with such a man or in a household where there are no women regularly in residence, this may lead to a crisis of cuisine. This problem can be solved by addressing the cooking-dining process with slapdash hamburgers and TV dinners, em-ploying household help, or eating out. These answers, however, for most of us range from unsatisfying to economically impossible or inconvenient.

Each of us and his wife has rejected such solutions. Our wives have almost always had demanding, full-time jobs and each couple has worked out arrangements to share the responsibility for prepar-ing meals. In one household the responsibility for marketing, plan-ning and cooking rotates between husband and wife every two weeks. In the other, the wife does not like to cook, except episodi-cally when she embarks on a spasm of activity involving mainly soups, beans and pastas. This, however, is too erratic to rely on for regular sustenance. She makes up for this defect by coping with

---

*We are aware that the title of this book strongly implies that the authors are liber-ated, i.e., free of the stereotypes we are about to mention. We also realize that as-serting this sort of liberation is like claiming to speak "frankly" and "honestly." The stronger one argues, the more others doubt.

kids, paying the bills, puzzling out inscrutable health insurance forms and repairing the vacuum cleaner, clothes dryer and other appliances which may be out of order. We do not offer either of these arrangements as models for work-sharing but rather as examples of the kind of participation by men that is necessary if women's liberation is not to mark the end of fine cooking on a regular basis.

For many who have full working lives, engaging in fine cooking requires another sort of liberation—from the intimidation of an "all or nothing" approach to gourmet cooking. We believe that more men—and probably women too—would participate with pleasure in preparing fine dishes if they thought they could produce impressive results without undue complexity and within a reasonable time. We believe this is possible and in this book present recipes that usually can be prepared in less than one hour. There are many dishes that taste and look much better than their preparation time would suggest. They offer the satisfaction of having really made good use of time in the kitchen. In fact, two or three courses (one or more from this book, sometimes with simple non-recipe fare, e.g., hamburger, rice, salad) or exquisite no-preparation courses (e.g., sausage, cheese, sashimi) can be prepared within that time. And while it is not our purpose to show how best to economize on meals, what we propose does not simply substitute dollars for effort.

Lawyers as Cookbook Editors? Brillat-Savarin, whose Physiology of Taste is the Everest of the literature of gastronomy (he wrote: "Tell me what you eat and I shall tell you what you are"), was a lawyer, counselor to Talleyrand and Judge of the Paris Court of Appeals. We have, since discovering these facts, felt secure in our kitchen avocation.

But, being lawyers has contributed more, we think, than that basis for self satisfaction. Some may find in these pages only evidence of our profession's turgid writing style, but we hope at least the lawyer's duty of punctilious drafting will enable the reader to avoid bafflement sometimes found in other kitchen manuals. We are reminded of one of our earliest encounters with a leading cookbook in which, part way through the directions for an elaborate Veal Valentino, appears the command "remove the veal"—the absolutely last reference to the veal. Only after a short physical struggle were we able to persuade the cook in charge that evening that the dish was not veal-flavored asparagus tips and mushrooms (sans veal) and that he should restore the veal to the pan before serving. Then there is the opaque (at least to us) reference which commences a recipe in another celebrated volume: "Prepare a pheasant in the usual manner."

Perhaps more significant than drafting precision is the lawyer's duty to present all the relevant and competing considerations but let the client make the decisions. ("A lawyer should exert his best efforts to insure that decisions of his [sic] client are made only after the client has been informed of relevant considerations." American Bar Association Code of Professional Responsibility EC7-8). We hope this book gives good advice that will enable users to decide for themselves what level of elegance-perfection they wish to achieve, taking account of the occasion for which they are cooking, availability of ingredients and how much time they have. Sometimes we suggest a sliding scale of excellence as well as variations that allow to the users their own initiative and imagination. With cookbook authors, as with doctors, lawyers and other professionals, we think it wrong not to involve the client in important decisions.

Whom Is It For? One of our major goals is to promote boldness in using limited time in the kitchen, and our hunch is that those who need this most are men like ourselves who, in their early working years, did not do much cooking thanks to a system that assigned that role to mothers, sisters and wives. But we hope many women with limited time to cook will also find the book provocative and useful.

One of the important dividends of impressive results for limited effort is that they may encourage participation by younger children* with limited patience and no interest in the ultimate niceties of haute-cuisine. This is particularly gratifying to working parents who may have the sense that, between their daytime schedule and the demands of their children's homework and evening telephone obligations, the twain rarely meet. Working in the kitchen together for an hour before dinner may offer a better chance to get caught up than the traditional "what happened in school today" and the equally traditional "nothing." Many of our exemplary recipes have

---

*Older children may collaborate on a higher level.

divisible units that can be assigned to kids and many can be prepared entirely by them while the father (or mother) does another.

Applying Cost-Benefit Theory. We believe that there are not
just two ways of preparing a particular dish—perfect or un-
worthy—but a graduated scale along which different levels of effort, money and, in some instances, unwanted cholesterol or
calories, produce better results. We recognize, of course, that not
every meal can require attention and care; circumstances will often
require something quick or cheap or both. At the other extreme,
we do not mean to discourage the application of infinite effort to a
culinary masterpiece, but that is not what this book is about. Ours
is the territory in between, and we show how modest expenditures
of effort over the minimum may produce impressive results.

Furthermore, by being conscious of how much kitchen time
produces what incremental results, meals can be planned in the
fullest sense of the word. For example, there are many instances in
which buying a partially prepared ingredient such as frozen
raspberries as sauce for fresh strawberries or poached peaches will
be both easier and cheaper than starting with the "real thing" (in
this case crushing and sugaring fresh raspberries) and will produce
a result that you will feel is as good or almost as good. Recipes for
the great Indian dish, chicken tandoori, for example, may call for a
whole roasting chicken and hours of marination. But boned chicken
breasts, which are enormously useful and versatile, cook more
quickly than dark meat, bone in, insulated by the bulk of the whole
bird. And perhaps identical flavor can be created by first stage
marination for 15 minutes, second stage baking, followed by broiling for three minutes. After a while it is natural to use hot marinations which penetrate more quickly than cold; thinly sliced ingredients which cook faster than big chunks. Also, stir frying comes
easily as a time-economical method of preparing many dishes. We
suggest how you may chop, simmer, prepare, etc. while other procedures are going on, e.g., boiling, chilling, etc. Similarly, stuffed
vegetables can be speeded along by parboiling while preparing
stuffing. Two things may therefore go on at once instead of in sequence. All these and other approaches to reducing kitchen time
are amplified and discussed in the recipes that follow.

Obviously, in this sort of book we cannot provide a complete, calibrated catalogue of levels of excellence or sacrifice related to all dishes or ingredients. We have tried to do some consciousness-raising by describing an approach to reducing kitchen time through some examples that reflect our own experiences. Much of the pleasure of cooking with dispatch, yet with panache, lies in evolving one's own scale—including, we hope, a minimum to which one never goes even in direst emergency—e.g., canned beef gravy.

A Modular Approach. There are many instances when mastering a particular basic ingredient will, in effect, provide the basis for a large variety of dishes. Take chicken breasts as an example. With different marinations and/or dusting with flour and/or spices, they can be sauteed and (1) covered with cheese and baked as chicken parmigiana; (2) presented on a provençal sauce; (3) prepared as a curry; (4) a Mexican casserole with green peppers; (5) made Chinese style with soy sauce and peanut butter; (6) Japanese style, fried with a dusting of flour and ginger; or (7) with a wine and mushroom sauce. The recipes, of course, are different, but soon you learn how to handle the main ingredient and how it responds to various marination, dusting, coating, saucing. Conversely, a curry technique (dusting with flour and curry powder before browning) can be used on chicken, lamb, shrimp, or beef. Or tandoori style treatment (marination followed by yogurt coating and broiling) may be accorded beef, chicken or fish. A first course of crudités goes well with at least a half dozen sauces or accompaniments (vinaigrette, aioli, anchovies, etc.), because fresh vegetables are vastly adaptable. And once ingredients for various sauces and flourings are on your shelves the same or similar approaches can be used for a variety of raw materials.

The module approach suggests a more deliberate way of dealing with leftovers. When it would appear to be efficient, we suggest that you prepare a double dose of the basic meat or fish component or of a sauce and refrigerate or freeze it, depending on the item and when you plan to use it next. It takes almost no additional time to prepare a larger amount and where, as will usually be the case, holding over half involves no deterioration in quality, it is something busy people should do, particularly if their lives are well enough organized so they can plan when they will use it. Incidentally, by preparing twice (or three times) what you think you will need for the first meal, you avoid being stuck with the awkward small leftover reflecting your desire not to come too close to the line in estimating appetites.

No-Preparation Elegance. In planning meals remember that one or two courses can rely for their elegance on imaginative marketing. Crudités, crisp, fresh vegetables in season, are colorful and fun with a variety of sauces or accompaniments; your shopping expeditions can turn up a great variety of sausages, which offered to those at the table for slicing make a colorful, exotic presentation. Steak tartare is largely prepared raw at the butcher, or in a moment at home. If you have a good fishmonger nearby, sashimi or various fish tartares are instantly yours. The most soigne of restaurants offer smoked Nova Scotia or Scotch salmon as a first course. Expensive, but a little goes a long way. An imaginative selection of cheeses and colorful fruits are a splendid way to follow an appetizer and main course involving some serious cooking.

Developing Courage, Flexibility and Imagination. In our culinary excursions, we found that the air of precision and definitiveness of most recipes stands in the way of serious cooking by busy people. Nothing can be worse than coming home full of resolve to prepare a particular dish and finding that you are out of olive oil or oregano or shallots and have to return to the market, or that you'd forgotten that you have to marinate the shrimp two hours. Or, something which would be great to do on a weekend and, indeed, fun, might seem impossible because a half dozen prescribed steps will consume hours. But recipes which pontificate—as many do—like many other of life's prescriptions, don't deserve mindless fealty. Maybe there's not much leeway in building a bridge (although even in bridge building there are options) but symphonies are played beautifully many ways and the same scene has been painted, even with genius, with considerable variety. After all, if the recipe writer had obtained his or her formula at a different restaurant, the peasant village down the road, another province or country, the olive oil might be butter, lard, margarine or vegetable oil. Some estimable gourmets insist upon olive oil; others equally revered say there is no good olive oil nowadays and a good peanut or vegetable oil is better; others make neater discriminations, matching oils (walnut, sesame) to other ingredients. For some experts the oregano should or could be thyme, marjoram, basil, other herbs or any combination thereof. The shallots might be onions, scallions, leeks. The marination might be for twenty minutes, 24 hours or omitted altogether in favor of mere baking or broiling in the marinade. Six step sequences often can be merged into two or three steps.

A glance at authoritative cookbooks convinces anyone that while you cannot say "Anything goes," there is scope for reasonable judgment. The same recipe varies considerably from one book to another and, with some changes, often converts from French to Italian or Spanish or Mexican, and so forth. We found an interesting example in three of Elizabeth David's books which we consulted on how to make bourride, the great Provençal fish dish. Having with us on vacation her Mediterranean Food, French Country Cooking and French Provincial Cooking, we haphazardly first looked in one; the next day in preparing for marketing, we picked up another; and in getting to work on the bourride in the kitchen, opened the third. There was some slight confusion as it became apparent that the first book, in prescribing ingredients for the court bouillon, called for lemon peel and white wine or vinegar. The second called for *orange peel*, white wine and vinegar. The third required wine vinegar and lemon peel. Instead of the onion prescribed in the first two, the third listed leeks. The recipe for the aioli, or mayonnaise with garlic, which is mixed with broth and spread on the fish, varied considerably among the recipes, but there is no point in setting all those differences forth here. And, as if to underscore the scope one has in matters of this sort, in French Provincial Cooking, she presents a recipe also for Potage de Poissons a la Nîmoise, which is a Languedoc version of bourride. In this, the court bouillon is different from that of the previous recipes in that it contains carrot, garlic, "parsley and whatever other herbs you happen to have, plus olive oil and seasonings." There are other differences too. Now, the three versions of bourride hardly represent carelessness by Mrs. David. She is among the great writers and scholars on the subject of food. There are indeed many ways of making the same dish and of altering it to become another equally delicious one. Just as Poissons a la Nîmoise is a permissible variation of bourride, we could compose Poissons a la Cambridge or San Francisco, adding or omitting regional, seasonal or other ingredients. Our creations would be somewhat different, but could be delicious. Since the theme of this book is speed and ease, selection of alternative ingredients could be made using those criteria.

One further observation. Until recently, fine cooking meant to most people French cooking. But now there is debate over whether other cuisines are indeed not superior to the French. Mexican, Chinese, Italian, Indian and other cuisines all offer possibilities that at least reach Gallic heights and we have drawn on our travels and restaurant-going as well as book research to suggest culinary efforts from all over the globe. We do not propose to judge the debate, only to suggest that it is fair to look in many directions before preparing one's table.

Whether proposing recipes within national cuisines or crossing international boundaries, we often will suggest variations which may be pursued if practicalities require it, or taste or whimsy so indicate. Generally, there are families of flavors and functions within which substitutions work. If you do not have one herb, a good guess is that many others will do. The peasants, fishermen and restaurateurs who conceived the standard repertory could have used one as well as another and usually did. Obviously, bacon fat and butter will give entirely different tastes. But to take an extreme possibility, if the recipe calls for one and you have only the other, you might want to use it and compensate with regard to other ingredients by using more or less salt or other flavoring. If you introduce bacon, you may get a smokey version of the basic dish. White wine, red wine, vermouth and sherry all have different flavors. If you are out of one, you might think through the entire recipe and imagine whether one of the others might do, as might lemon juice or vinegar. Onions, shallots, leeks, scallions, chives are related in flavor, and the outcome of using them will be different. They substitute readily for one another; ditto for sour cream, yogurt, or sometimes sweet cream. We do not suggest that the result will be the same. The differences, however, all may be interesting and rarely objectionable. Usually such switches will work, and when they do, you might keep the dish in your repertory and rename it appropriately.

The same goes for the various oils (vegetable, olive), butters (salt, sweet), chicken, goose or duck fat (which you might have left over and wonder how to use), etc. For example, classic Mexican recipes often call for lard which we don't like and so we generally use something else, usually butter or olive oil. And speaking of Mexican cooking, if you tamper with many dishes from other cuisines by adding peppers and herbs typically found in Mexican cooking, you may stumble on a result which you might find in Mexico. While you should be prepared for disappointment or disaster, experimentation and innovation usually pay off.

Assumptions re Time and Equipment. Our pledge is that almost any dish here can be prepared within an hour, usually far less, so that entire meals can be composed in under an hour. In a few instances, some of this time will have to be invested during the evening or morning preceding final preparation, as where ingredients must be chilled. Where this is necessary, it is clearly flagged in the recipe. Of course, it sometimes may be more convenient to prepare part of a meal a day or two in advance. For example, while you are waiting for tonight's dinner to cook or while family or friends are cleaning up, you may have a few minutes in which you can prepare ceviche, oranges givres or a macedoine of fresh fruit for the next meal. Again, this requires a bit of planning, but planning is essential if people with other demands are to have interesting meals and have it be a pleasure not a burden.

This book does not assume you have an elaborate kitchen. Because we guess many homes have a blender or food processor our recipes do make reference to such processes.

Special thanks to Daniel Halberstam, Lynnette Lee Villanueva and Aaron Brenner for their help in typing, composing and other matters.

Menu Suggestions

Following, by way of examples, are a number of menus one may put together out of this book. We have, out of a sense of orderliness, assembled them according to national origin. But, surely, in actual meal preparation, one may mix and match ethnicities according to taste and convenience.

The times given are in five minute modules. All of the courses, of course, need not be served in a simple meal. Several processes may go on at once, e.g., boiling water for pasta and making salad dressing.

Mexico　　　　Ceviche—15 minutes preparation, 40 minutes chilling
Chicken Mole—15 minutes preparation, 20 minutes cooking
Lime shells filled with lime sorbet (limes givres)

China (with Moroccan dessert)
Cold noodles with peanut sauce—10 minutes preparation, 10 minutes cooking
Chicken with red and green peppers—5 minutes preparation, 10 minutes cooking
Fresh orange slices Fez

Japan　　　　Gomo-ae (chilled stringbeans with sesame dressing) 10 minutes preparation (if fresh, less if frozen), 5 minutes cooking
Tastaage Japanese fried chicken—10 minutes preparation, 10 minutes cooking
Fresh pineapple—10 minutes preparation

Italy　　　　Small shells primavera with hazel nuts or walnuts— 10 minutes preparation, 10 minutes cooking
Tomato and mozzarella salad—5 minutes preparation

Chicken strips with lemon sauce—5 minutes preparation, 10 minutes cooking
Gorgonzola cheese and honey (no preparation)

France   Assorted sausages and mustards—5 minutes preparation
Nearly instant bouillabaisse—15 minutes preparation, 20 minutes cooking
Mixed green salad garnished with chevre on onion slices—10 minutes preparation
Oranges givres—10 minutes preparation

India   Vegetable pakhoras—10-15 minutes
Blue fish tandoori—15 minutes preparation, 25 minutes cooking
Fresh fruit—zero time

American Crudités with vinaigrette—15 minutes
Texas Chili with chocolate—35 minutes
Apple crisp—15 minutes preparation, 30 minutes baking

CHAPTER II

Appetizers

Mainly, these appetizers rely on getting high quality fresh ingredients, preparing them with little or no cooking, using the freezer to chill quickly, when called for, or, when cooking, using stir frying techniques. Our version of ceviche, for example, telescopes the hours which some recipes require (in some versions a day or more of marinating) into 30 minutes by using finely chopped fish and combining with hot marinade to accelerate the penetration and mingling of flavors, followed by chilling in the deep freeze (but, of course, not freezing). We also chill chicken liver pate in the freezer. Raw fish preparations, guacamole and avocado margarita (our invention) require no cooking at all. Sausages require virtually no preparation. Mexican shrimp hash relies on quick stir frying. Some other appetizers require more effort, but come in at well under one hour, easily, leaving time to prepare other courses, if you choose to make a multi-course, elaborate meal.

All of these appetizers may be served with cocktails. Larger portions of some may be served as main courses or used to stuff vegetables.

Almost Instant Ceviche
(Preparation time: 15 minutes chopping, mixing;
30-40 minutes chilling)

Serves 4–6

> 1 lb. of any of the following: fresh filet of sole, blue fish,
>   striped bass, mackerel, shelled shrimp, or scallops
>   (bay or ocean), or combination of two or more
>   thereof.
> fresh lime or lemon juice to cover (a cup or somewhat less)
> 2 ozs. olive or vegetable oil
> 1 chile serrano or a tsp. finely chopped jalapeno or other hot
>   pepper (or 3-4 dashes tabasco)
> 1 small tomato, chopped
> 1 medium size onion, chopped
> 1 large or two small cloves garlic finely chopped
> salt
> ground black pepper

Optional:
> 2 tbsps. chopped fresh cilantro (known also as fresh coriander
>   or chinese parsley) or ⅛ tsp. grated orange peel or
>   2 tbsps. chopped fresh Italian parsley

Cut the fish into tiny pieces, i.e., approximately ⅛″ cubes.
Place in a heatproof glass or ceramic dish, the larger and flatter the
better. A large pyrex pie plate is perfect. Add onion, garlic, tomato,
chile or tabasco, optional cilantro, or grated orange peel or parsley,
salt and pepper to taste. Simmer the lime juice and oil for a minute, pour over the fish and other ingredients. Mix together, allow
to cool for five to ten minutes. Place uncovered in freezer until
chilled (after 15 minutes, check every 10 minutes to make sure it is
not freezing). Remove from freezer and place in refrigerator until
ready to serve. Mix together once more and serve. A pretty presentation is on a lettuce leaf, perhaps in a large wine glass, or on a
plate, garnished with an avocado slice and a couple of red radishes
and olives.

Commentary:

A few years ago, we traveled through Mexico together enjoying the varied cuisines, rarely seen north of the border, where Mexican food almost always means Tex-Mex. In the coastal areas (and in some interior cities with access to the coast) we sampled ceviche made with all sorts of fish and shellfish. This recipe is one adaptation of what we experienced.

Typical ceviche recipes marinate overnight or at least for a few hours. Mincing the fish fine and covering with hot lime juice accelerates the process: the marinade does not have as far to penetrate, the hot lime juice draws the flavors from the various ingredients and unifies them more rapidly than if both were cold, the conventional mode of marination. The cilantro is extraordinarily good, some would say essential, but you may have to hunt for it. There is a dried version on supermarket shelves but it is nearly tasteless. Fresh parsley is a substitute for cilantro in appearance but not flavor. The orange peel option is a nice, but unusual, variation. If you use it, use only the surface of the peel.

Ceviche can be prepared a couple of days in advance. In this event, fine mincing, heating the marinade and use of the freezer is unnecessary—just refrigerate. Use larger chunks, ½" cubes or larger. The fish which we have specified in the list of ingredients are exemplary; any other type may be tried. But we would avoid codfish and oilier species.

Meatballs Caracas
(Preparation time: 15 minutes)

Serves 4–6

1 lb. ground lean beef
2 tbsps. cumin
3 cloves garlic
salt
ground fresh pepper

Chop garlic. Mix all ingredients together. Form about 20

meatballs, each the size of a large marble or small ping-pong ball. Heat a large frying pan and place meatballs in it. They will begin sautéing in their own fat. The pan should be large enough to leave space among the meatballs to facilitate turning. Therefore, if the pan is not large enough, cook them in two shifts. Turn with a spatula or large spoon until brown on all sides (6-8 minutes). Pour off fat and serve hot.

Commentary:

At a United Nations Congress on the Prevention of Crime and Treatment of Offenders in Caracas in 1980, one of us was a guest at a party given for the delegates in a VIP lounge at the Caracas race-track. The food was generally unnoteworthy except for the meat-balls, which, however, were terrific. We think we have faithfully replicated, or perhaps improved upon the original.

Pimentos and Anchovies George Bizos
(Preparation time: 45 minutes; 15-20 minutes charring peppers,
15-20 minutes cooking, 10 minutes cutting and other preparation)

> **4 red bell peppers (green and yellow or mixed colors may be substituted; a multi-colored dish is extremely attractive)**
> **1 tin (or better, a jar) anchovies**
> **2 ozs. olive oil**
> **2-3 garlic cloves (optional)**
> **3 tbsps. red wine vinegar**
> **oregano (pinch)**

Place peppers under broiler and turn every 3-4 minutes until they are charred on all sides. Place in a closed paper bag while they cool, for perhaps 20 minutes. Place anchovies in wine vinegar while peppers cook and cool. When peppers cool, remove charred skin, stem and seeds, cut into strips 1-2″ wide. Arrange strips on a platter. On each strip, place an anchovy filet. Dribble olive oil over

the dish. (Slice garlic if you use it and sprinkle over dish). Sprinkle
oregano over all. Serve with crusty French or Italian bread.

Commentary:

George Bizos is a South African advocate (barrister) who has
represented defendants in many celebrated political trials. He was
born in Greece and presents a fabulous Greek cuisine at his home
near Johannesburg. His whole roasted lamb turned on a spit all day
doesn't fit the formula of this book. The anchovies he uses in making this dish, of course, are not canned, but the salted variety
which he bones and marinates himself in vinegar and olive oil.
Since salted whole anchovies are difficult to find and time consuming to filet, we use the common canned or jarred anchovy. But we
preserve his marination in vinegar, a rare treatment, which imparts
a particularly agreeable flavor.

Goma-ae
Cold stringbeans and sesame sauce—Japanese
(Preparation time: 15 minutes)

Serves 4–6

1 lb. stringbeans (preferably fresh, but frozen will do)
2 tbsps. sesame seeds
4 tbsps. sake or sherry
¼ tsp. sugar
1 tbsp. soy sauce
salt to taste

Trim stringbeans, if fresh. If they are very long, cut in half.
Bring salted water to boil. Boil beans in water 6-7 minutes, less if
frozen, cool under running water until chilled.
While water and beans are boiling, toast sesame seeds by placing in a frying pan over high heat, shaking occasionally. *As soon as*
they begin turning darker, remove from heat. This should take

3-5 minutes. Place seeds in blender with sake, soy sauce and sugar. Blend until seeds are somewhat crunched or broken up. Alternatively, the mixture could be pulverized with a mortar and pestle. A food processor might be used, but our experience has been that there isn't enough material for the processor to come to grips with, and the stuff quickly adheres to the side of the processor, evading the blade.

Pour the mixture over the stringbeans. Refrigerate until ready to serve.

Commentary:

This one of our favorite Japanese appetizers served at Fuji, a New York Japanese restaurant, where we got the recipe.

Guacamole
(Preparation time: under 15 minutes)

Serves 4

> 1 ripe avocado
> 1 small onion chopped
> 1 clove garlic chopped finely
> juice of 1 lime or lemon
> 1 small chile serrano, chopped, or ½ tsp. of some other hot
>   pepper, chopped or several dashes tabasco several
>   sprigs chopped cilantro (also called Chinese parsley
>   or fresh coriander)
> 1 ripe tomato (or two small canned plum tomatoes) chopped

Mash avocado with a fork. Mix together all ingredients. Serve on a lettuce leaf or as a dip with tostadas, corn chips, crackers, fresh vegetables, etc. Guacamole is a delicious stuffing for chilled tomatoes or large mushroom caps.

Commentary:

The cilantro is particularly good for guacamole but in many places not readily available. As noted in the ceviche recipe dried cilantro is nearly tasteless. Parsley resembles it in appearance but not in flavor.

There are many variations of guacamole. Some leave out the tomato or onion or garlic or cilantro or hot pepper or various combinations of the above. Some skin and seed the tomato. Often we use canned tomatoes which in some seasons are superior to fresh. Some add a bit of oil or mayonnaise, but since the avocado is oily, this seems excessive. Finely chopped green or red sweet peppers (1 tbsp.) are a nice addition for color. An ⅛ tsp. grated orange rind (only the thin outer layer) in lieu of cilantro provides an interesting variation.

Other variations of which we have read are to add a couple of tbsps. of white wine or a few drops of Worcestershire. But we have never wanted to taste guacamole made with either. Both would seem to be grossly unauthentic.

Our fondest guacamole recollection is of Oaxaca. We purchased the ingredients in the local market and prepared the guacamole on the window sill of our second floor hotel room facing the zocalo (town square). As we chopped and stirred, sipping Margaritas, Mexican serape vendors displayed their wares beneath our window, led by several who recalled our interest, expressed casually earlier in the day, in a serape with butterfly designs. Dozens of colorful serapes embroidered with mariposas (butterflies) were spread on the sidewalk. Altogether a perfect combination.

Avocado Margaritas
(Preparation time: under 15 minutes)

Serves 4

> 1 ripe avocado
> 2-3 ozs chopped almonds (quantity proportionate to size of
>   avocado)
> 1 oz tequila
> 1 oz lemon juice
> salt, pepper

Mash avocado. Toast almonds lightly in a pan over a medium flame. Add to avocado. Thoroughly stir in tequila, lemon juice. Serve as you would guacamole.

Commentary:

Why consume the avocado and Margarita separately? This is our alternative version of guacamole. But it will not keep for long, even in the refrigerator. After an hour or so, the almonds become soggy and the tequila and avocado separate. So consume soon after it is prepared.

Steak Tartare
(Preparation time: under 15 minutes)

Serves 4

> 1 lb. freshly ground very lean steak
> 1 jar or tin anchovies, drained of oil, chopped
> 2 tbsps. capers
> 1 medium chopped onion, preferably sweet, or 4-5 chopped
>   scallions
> Dijon or other mustard; powdered mustard (in very modest
>   quantity) may be used instead
> Worcestershire
> 1 tbsp. chopped chile peppers or several drops of tabasco
>   sauce
> salt
> freshly ground pepper
> 1 raw egg (optional)

If you are using the egg, mix egg and meat thoroughly. Keep meat (with or without egg) chilled until ready to serve. Place all ingredients in separate bowls so that each participant may mix them and ground steak together on his or her individual plate to taste.

Serve preferably with thin black bread; crisp crackers or rye bread will do.

Commentary:

We prefer to omit the egg, although it serves as a glue, holding the ingredients together better. Some prefer to place the egg in boiling water one minute before mixing. Each person mixing his or her own enables the participant to prepare the dish to individual taste (e.g., with more or less onion, mustard, chile pepper). But all the ingredients could be mixed together in advance in a serving bowl. As usual, reasonable variations are possible. Some omit the Worcestershire, tabasco or chopped hot chile peppers and/or mustard. Steak tartare sometimes is a main course, garnished with tomatoes, olives, radishes, etc. served on a bed of lettuce.

RAW FISH PREPARATIONS
(Preparation time: 15–20 minutes)

Japan

Chopped Tuna Gen

Serves 6

1 lb. fresh tuna fish
2 tbsps. finely chopped onion
½ tsp. wasabi (if unavailable use chopped horseradish)
1 tbsp. soy sauce
1 oz. caviar
2 tbsp. sesame seeds
1 cup finely chopped watercress or lettuce

Mince tuna fish finely with a knife or a cleaver. The food processor will turn it into a paste, which you do not want. If wasabi, Japanese horseradish which can be bought in most Asian food stores isn't available, American horseradish will do—the dish will taste different but in no way inferior. As to caviar, use the best you can afford, but luxury caviars, i.e. beluga or sevruga, are not necessary. Whitefish caviar will do as will salmon eggs, or indeed, the inexpensive lumpfish eggs. Mix tuna, wasabi or horseradish, onion and caviar. Toast sesame seeds in a frying pan or in a toaster oven with high heat until they begin to turn color. Then remove from heat. Place a bed of chopped watercress or lettuce on each plate and place a portion of the tuna mixture on it. Refrigerate until ready to serve. Sprinkle sesame seeds on tuna mixture. Serve.

Commentary:

We first had this dish at Gen, in Roppongi, Tokyo, and have replicated it many times. Great with sake or chilled vodka or akvavit.

France

Tuna and Sole Hache

Serves 6

½ lb. fresh tuna fish
½ lb. filet of sole or flounder
1 or 2 lemons cut into wedges

Chop tuna and sole (or flounder) separately, quite fine. Use a knife or sharp cleaver—the food processor may make mush.

Serve a dollop of each, maybe on a lettuce leaf, for each guest, who will squeeze his or her own lemon over the red and white mounds to taste. We had the dish in Paris but could have found it anywhere.

Spain

Chopped Sea Bass

Serves 6

1 lb. filet of sea bass
2 tbsps. finely chopped parsley
1 or 2 lemons cut into wedges

Chop sea bass quite fine with a knife or sharp cleaver. The food processor may make mush. Mix with parsley. Serve. Guests squeeze lemon wedges over fish to taste. From Madrid, but hardly exclusive to that city.

Mexican Shrimp Hash
(Preparation time: under 30 minutes, much less if shrimp is already peeled)

Serves 4–6

1 lb. fresh shrimp
1 small onion
2 cloves garlic
1 stick celery
1 small sweet red pepper
1 small chile serrano or equivalent (or few dashes tabasco)
4 tbsps. oil
handful fresh cilantro (optional)
salt, pepper

Peel and chop shrimp; chop very fine the onion, garlic, celery, sweet red pepper, chile serrano. Heat oil, add onion, garlic, red pepper, chile. Sauté together over medium heat 5 minutes until onion is soft. Add shrimp. Stir rapidly over high heat until shrimp begins to brown slightly. Add celery and continue stirring for a moment or two until it is heated through. Add salt and pepper to taste. Chop and add cilantro, if you are using it.

Commentary:

This may be made with crabmeat also, which nowadays is terribly expensive. Scallops (bay or sea—cut into small pieces) also are good. It may be used as a stuffing for precooked mushroom caps (sauté them first over high heat in oil for about five minutes) or tomatoes. Bake the scooped out tomato stuffed with cooked hash at 350 degrees for 10 minutes.

Assorted Sausages

Delicious, varied, full of surprises, ready in an instant, if served cold, not requiring much cooking if served hot, sometimes the product of pleasant meandering among ethnic butcher shops, groceries and delicatessens, sausages make an unusual and rewarding first course. French restaurants occasionally serve saucisson en croute, or sliced saucisse as an appetizer. Antipasto often includes thin sliced hard salami. Entrees of sausages are not uncommon (broiled, sautéed, in various preparations, e.g., choucroute, or lyonnais, etc.). Recently, there has been a resurgence of interest in sausages.

In any event, this is only by way of suggesting that there is a rich lode to be mined and great adventure in examining the endless variety of sausages, French, Italian, German, Hungarian, Mexican, English, Jewish, Chinese and other. Hormel markets a large variety nationally.

A good way to get into the subject is by serving sausages of various sorts, hot and cold, as appetizers. We have been served as many as two dozen kinds at once (at La Ferme in Villefranche near Nice which we visited several times during a month-long stay at

Eze Village on the Cote d'Azur), from a large basket, as one would serve crudités.

Three or four sausages as a first course will do. Served on a cutting board, with a sharp knife or knives, pickles or cornichons, a variety of mustards, and black or rye bread, or a good crusty French bread, they make a smashing first course.

With slightly more effort, you can lead off with one or two kinds of hot sausage (simmered for five minutes after having been punctured with a fork to let the fat run out, then browned in chopped onion which first has been sautéed five minutes; a sprinkling of caraway seeds is good on white sausages) followed by a selection of cold ones.

We are deliberately unspecific. Try a few different ones each time. It will be years before you exhaust the possibilities.

Sweetbread Tapas
(Preparation time: 15-20 minutes, excluding presoaking)

1 lb. sweetbreads
4 tbsps. vegetable or olive oil
4 cloves garlic
handful fresh parsley

Soak sweetbreads in cold water in refrigerator overnight or at least for several hours. Frequently they are available only frozen; if so, the defrosting can take place in water overnight. (One can readily construct a lawyer's argument to demonstrate that soaking time should not be computed as preparation time, constituting violation of our under-1-hour preparation pledge—but the dish is so good, unusual and easy to make, the rule should be waived anyway.) Trim away membranes and tubes. Place in boiling water for 5 minutes. Cut into small, thumbnail size pieces. Chop parsley fine. Chop garlic. Heat oil. Brown garlic in oil. Add sweetbread pieces. Stir as they brown on all sides. Toss chopped parsley over. Serve very hot.

Commentary:

In Spain, tapas bars serve tapas (snacks) and drinks during early evening before dinner, or if you eat enough of them, as dinner. The sweetbread tapas is one of our favorites.

Salmon Crudo Marinado Las Huertas
(Preparation time: 15 minutes)

Serves 6

1 lb. filet of fresh salmon
4 oz. olive oil
4 oz. lemon juice
2 shallots
1 small tomato

Slice salmon into very thin slices (1/16" if possible). It slices readily if slightly hardened, but not frozen, in the freezer. Chop shallots and tomato, squeeze lemons, pour shallots, tomato, lemon juice and oil over salmon slices. Marinate 5 minutes. (The salmon can marinate longer, if that fits your schedule. It is firmest and tastes best, however, after brief marination).

Commentary:

In Santiago de Compostelo, Spain, there is a marvelous restaurant—Las Huertas—at which this is a terrific specialty. It is not only delicious, but when the slices are spread out to cover the serving dish, makes a beautiful presentation.

Joyce Georges's Fish Cakes
(Preparation time: 20 minutes)

Serves 4–6

1 lb. filleted flounder or sea bass or cod (other fish will do)
2 tbsps. flour
1 tsp. baking powder
2 tbsps. chopped chives (other herbs will do)
1 tsp. chopped hot jalapeño pepper
4 tbsps. vegetable oil

Chop fish to a pulp—the big blade of food processor is most efficient way. Add remaining ingredients, mix well together. Form fish cakes 2–3″ in diameter, ½″ thick. Heat oil in pan. Sauté on one side until brown—turn over and brown on other. Serve.

Commentary:

The Honorable Telford Georges has been (believe it or not) a Chief Justice of the Supreme Courts of Trinidad and Tobago, the Bahamas, Belize, Bermuda, Tanzania and Zimbabwe. He now is on the Supreme Court of the Bahamas and is a member of the Privy Council. We once dined at his home in Harare where his wife, Joyce, made these fishcakes of Caribbean and African provenance as a cocktail snack.

Cold Noodles Oriental Style

(Preparation time: 20 minutes to boil water; 3–5 minutes to cook noodles; 10 minutes, while water is boiling, to make sauce; 15 minutes to chill)

Serves 6

1 lb. thin linguine or other thin noodle. If Chinese rice noodles or Japanese buckwheat noodles are available, they are preferable.

1 large pot, approximately six quarts

8 ozs. chicken broth (canned or made from bouillon powder or cubes)

2 ozs. soy sauce

4 ozs. vinegar or 2 fresh limes or lemons

2 cloves garlic

2 tsps. powdered ginger or 3 tsps. grated fresh ginger

¼ tsp. cumin seed

2 tbsps. peanut or vegetable oil

1 small sweet red pepper

2–4 dashes tabasco

4 tbsps. peanut butter, preferably with bits of peanuts in it

2 ozs. sesame oil

Fill pot ¾ full of water. Add 2–3 tbsps. salt. Bring to boil. Add noodles and cook until *al dente* (about as hard as can be while still edible). To accomplish this, consult cooking time on box and taste a noodle when half that time has passed. If not done, cook another minute or two and try again. As soon as a noodle is edible, remove them from pot and place under cold running water until chilled. They should be done in 5–7 minutes, although the instructions on the box may tell you to boil the noodles 10 minutes or more.

While water is boiling, prepare sauce: chop garlic and red pepper. Squeeze limes or lemons. Heat peanut or vegetable oil over medium high flame. Sauté garlic and red pepper for 3–4 minutes in oil. Add chicken broth and, except for peanut butter, remaining ingredients. Bring to simmer. Add peanut butter and stir until it dissolves. Simmer for 3–5 minutes to thicken sauce.

Place noodles in as large a flat pyrex dish as you can find. The idea is to have as much surface area as possible. Pour sauce over noodles, mix thoroughly, place in freezer for fifteen minutes to chill. Check to make sure noodles don't freeze. If not chilled, remove, toss, return to freezer and leave noodles there somewhat longer, until chilled. Then place in refrigerator covered with plastic wrap until ready to serve. Mix sauce and noodles again thoroughly. Dribble sesame oil over before serving. Mei Yan, a Chinese friend, has taught us not to cook with the sesame oil because the heat causes it to lose its fragrance. However, dribbling it over a dish before serving maximizes its flavor. Some like the dish very spicy. If so, add spicy sesame oil before serving or increase quantity of ginger and chilies.

Chicken Liver Pâté
(Preparation time: 30 minutes including 15 minutes in freezer)

Serves 4

    4 chicken livers
    4 tbsps. butter
    1 small onion
    ¼ tsp. thyme
    ⅛ tsp. nutmeg
    1 tsp. cognac
    ½ tsp. salt, freshly ground pepper
    1 tbsp. chopped parsley

Chop onion. Trim chicken livers, cutting away veins and extraneous tissue. Cut livers into eighths. Melt butter, sauté onions five minutes over medium high heat, stirring occasionally. They should become soft and golden in color. Add chicken livers, stir occasionally three-four more minutes. Mix in thyme, nutmeg, salt, pepper. Pour into blender or food processor. Add cognac. Process until entirely smooth, stopping occasionally and scraping mixture down from side of container.

Spread out on a flat pyrex or other temperature resistant plate. Place in freezer for fifteen minutes. This should chill it well. Remove from this dish and place in small serving container. Sprinkle parsley on top. Serve with crackers or toast.

Commentary:

With some slight variations, you could make "Jewish" chopped liver. Follow the same procedure, but omit thyme, nutmeg and cognac. If chicken fat is available, use it instead of butter. Mash a hard boiled egg and with a fork, mix into the chopped liver. This mixture should not be as smooth as the pâté.

Pakhoras
(Preparation time: 10–30 minutes depending on choice of ingredients)

Pakhoras are little Indian pancakes which incorporate an infinite choice of other ingredients—vegetables, seafood, meat or combinations thereof. The batter and cooking methods vary too. For simplicity we propose starting out with peas or cauliflower cut into small pieces, small bits of chicken or small shrimp, or, for that matter, almost any leftover meat or vegetables. We have seen batters of flour and water only (best for a beginner), flour, water and egg and with or without baking powder. We have seen them fried in a pan until brown or deep fried. Curry powder, or your own mixture of a pinch of ginger, cumin, turmeric and perhaps cayenne pepper should be mixed with the flour. Add water until the flour and curry flavoring is sticky but not runny. Fold in vegetables, chicken or shrimp. Heat oil in frying pan. Place a tablespoon of batter for each pancake in hot oil. When edges begin to brown, turn over. Cook until both sides are golden. Serve.

Chinese Beef Package
(Preparation time: 20–30 minutes)

Serves 6

1 head of Boston, iceberg or other large leaf lettuce
1 lb. ground beef (pork is equally good)
1 medium onion
1 medium green pepper
2 cloves garlic
2 tsps. chopped fresh ginger (or 1 tsp. powdered ginger)
3 ozs. soy sauce
3 ozs. vinegar (rice vinegar preferable, but any will do)
4 ozs. walnuts (pecans or almonds will do)
2 tbsps. peanut or vegetable oil
2 ozs. sesame oil

Brown beef in a frying pan over a high flame. Pour off fat, place beef aside on a plate while cooking remainder of ingredients. Chop onion, pepper, garlic, nuts, ginger. Add oil to pan and heat over medium flame. Brown nuts, remove and set aside. Sauté garlic for 2–3 minutes, add onion and pepper and sauté for 5 minutes. Add soy sauce, vinegar, ginger and garlic, simmer 5 more minutes over low flame. Add meat, stir, cook 2–3 minutes more. Add nuts. Dribble sesame oil over.

Lift large untorn leaves off lettuce. Rinse. Dry in salad spinner or with paper towels.

Serve meat mixture in one bowl, lettuce leaves on a plate. Place a spoon or two (depending on size of leaf) of meat mixture in a leaf, fold over into a package and eat holding package between fingers.

Commentary:

The otherwise rightfully disparaged iceberg lettuce is strong enough to hold the meat without tearing. Its crispness (and lack of distinct flavor) is a nice contrast to the hot, spicy meat. Swiss chard leaves do nicely in this dish, too.

Turnip Pancakes
(Preparation time: 15 minutes)

Serves 4–6

½ lb. turnips
1 medium onion
1 red pepper
1 clove garlic
2 tbsps. chopped hot pepper
½ cup flour
½ cup sour cream
½ lb. salmon caviar
2 tbsps. salt
6 tbsps. vegetable oil

Julienne turnips into matchstick size pieces, using food processor or grater. Place in colander and mix with salt. (As the rest of the work goes on the turnips will exude water.) Julienne red pepper and onion. Chop hot pepper very fine. Mince garlic very fine and brown in the oil. Turn off flame. Remove the garlic. Squeeze the julienned turnip in your fist, forcing out liquid. Then mix the turnip, onion, red pepper, hot pepper and flour in a large mixing bowl. The flour will make the mixture sticky. On a flat surface form very thin, 3 inch diameter pancakes. Heat oil. Lift pancakes with a spatula and gently place in hot oil, gently turning when edges brown. When both sides are golden remove, place on paper towels to absorb excess oil. While successive batches are browning, keep those which are done on a serving plate in warm oven. Serve. Each guest should place a dollop of sour cream and another of caviar on each pancake.

Hot Stuffed Mushrooms
(Preparation time: 10 minutes; cooking time: 20 minutes)

Serves 4

12 large mushrooms
2 tbsps. olive oil
1 small onion, chopped
½ clove garlic
4 anchovy filets, chopped
1 tbsp. chopped parsley
¼ tsp. salt
½ tsp. pepper
1 slice bread, soaked in water and squeezed dry
1 egg
1 tbsp. bread crumbs
1 tbsp. olive oil (additional)

Cut off stems of mushrooms and wash very well. Chop the stems and sauté in olive oil with onion and garlic for 5 minutes. Add anchovies, parsley, salt and pepper and cook 5 minutes longer over brisk flame. Remove from stove, add bread and egg and mix together until smooth.

Fill each mushroom cap with stuffing, rounding stuffing on top. Sprinkle with bread crumbs and 1 tbsp. olive oil, place in greased baking dish in hot oven (400 degrees) for 10 minutes.

Commentary:

Stuffed vegetables make a colorful delicious first course. Additional recipes appear in Chapter IX, Vegetables.

CHAPTER III

Crudités, Salads & Dressings

Crudités
*(Preparation time: under 25 minutes for
washing, arranging, blanching, if required)*

Fresh vegetables served raw (crudités), with or without dressing or garnish, make a simple, refreshing first course. Harder specimens, e.g., cauliflower or carrots, might be blanched, i.e. boiled a few minutes *only*, to make them slightly tender, then removed from the water and plunged into cold water to stop the cooking process. We suggest several sauces below into which the crudités may be dipped. While they may be presented whole in a bowl or basket or on a platter, (after having been washed, scraped and trimmed), allowing each diner to pare and slice portions at the table, this results in shards, stems and seeds which some prefer to get rid of in advance. If you are that fastidious, trim, remove seeds and stems and cut into manageable segments before serving. Sandier specimens (e.g., lettuce, spinach, mushrooms) require extra careful rinsing. Some purists say wipe, never wash mushrooms because they absorb a great deal of water, but we have never taken the time.

We have served bouquets of red, green and yellow peppers, tomatoes, celery, fennel, broccoli, carrots (smaller the better), lettuces (a.b.i., i.e., anything but iceberg), spinach (leaving enough stem to hold onto while dipping into a sauce), scallions (has radicchio's time come and gone, along with the kiwi?), mushrooms, cauliflower, etc.

With crudités, a variety of sauces and/or garnishes are possible; some are listed on pages 21, 47, 48, 49, and 50, in the section describing dressings, including vinaigrette, aioli, bagna cauda, sauce orientale, guacamole, anchovies, chopped olives. You might drape an anchovy filet over a carrot or celery stick, for example, or scoop up finely chopped olive in the hollow of a celery stick.

Introduction to Salads

Salad, like everything else in cuisine, is the subject of controversy. Some look down their noses at those who serve the salad before the main course, instead of after. For others, the best one might say of such a practice is that the perpetrators come from California. Californians, we think we have observed, while firm in their belief that salad comes first, do not yet look down on easterners for engaging in the odd practice of serving salad afterwards. While we are writing for a national audience, we take a stand on the salad issue: mixed green salads follow the main course, accompanied by cheeses.

Here we list a number of salads other than the customary mixed greens which are, we think, self-evident. Best, we believe, are a combination of lettuces, combined with watercress, or arugola, or endive (alone or in combination), with dressing and/or garnish as indicated below. A few of the salads in this section (not the mixed greens, of course) qualify for first course or main course treatment as you prefer.

Mexican Salad
(Preparation time: 15 minutes, scrubbing, peeling, slicing; 15–20 minutes parboiling, cooking, tossing)

Serves 4–6

2 medium zucchini
½ lb. stringbeans
6 small new potatoes (or fewer large ones, first cut into small
      potato sized chunks)
1 medium red onion
2 ripe peaches (pears or apples)
1 ripe avocado
1 pomegranate (if in season)
4 ozs. vinaigrette (it is better if highly seasoned, i.e. heavy
      on the mustard and garlic) (see p. 47)

Scrub zucchini to remove sand which clings to skin even when you can't see it. Cut lengthwise into spear shaped eighths. (If zucchini is very long, cut spears in half.) Trim ends off stringbeans; if very long, cut in half. Slice potatoes into ¼″–½″ slices. Bring water to a boil in 4 qt. pot. Lower zucchini in a strainer into water, add stringbeans and potatoes to pot. Add peaches. If using pears or apples, do not subject them to this process. As soon as water boils remove peaches with a slotted spoon and place under cold running water until cooled. (They have been placed in hot water to facilitate skinning.) Remove zucchini after one minute, place under cold water. With a slotted spoon, remove stringbeans after 5 minutes have elapsed, place under cold water. Remove potatoes after twelve minutes. Peel peach (or other fruit), slice into thin slices. Peel onion, slice into thin slices. Place all ingredients except avocado and pomegranate seeds in a salad bowl. Pour vinaigrette over. Place in freezer, uncovered, for 15 minutes. Peel avocado, slice and place in salad bowl. Open pomegranate, remove seeds, sprinkle on salad. Toss. Refrigerate until ready to serve.

Commentary:

If all of the prescribed ingredients are not available, you may use substitutes, e.g., cauliflower flowerlets or broccoli or other vegetables which should be briefly boiled. Yellow or sweet onion may be used instead of red onion. Nectarines may be used instead of other fruit. Seeded or seedless grapes may be added or substituted for peaches or pears. If the avocado is sliced long before placing in the salad, it should be covered with lemon juice to prevent becoming discolored. Same for apples or pears. If pomegranates are out of season (they are available in late summer and fall), they may be omitted. If you like the pomegranate seeds as we do, you may freeze a quantity for use during the year. Two pomegranates provide more than enough seeds for a year. We have been unable to find any frozen or canned in the stores.

Mozzarella and Tomato Salad
(Preparation time: Under 15 minutes)

Serves 4–6

1 lb. fresh mozzarella cheese (buffalo mozzarella is best)
1 lb. ripe tomatoes
12–18 anchovy filets
4 tbsps. wine vinegar
4 tbsps. very good olive oil

Drain oil from anchovy filets, place them in a dish with vinegar. Slice mozzarella and tomatoes into thin slices. Arrange in serving platter alternately, each slice partly overlapping the next. Cover each slice of tomato with an anchovy filet. Dribble olive oil over.

Commentary:

During successive summers, each of us spent several weeks as scholar-in-residence at Villa Serbelloni, a study center maintained by the Rockefeller Foundation in Bellagio, Italy, on Lake Como. Among the excellent items on the menus was this salad which is extraordinarily easy to make. Since we first saw it there it has been showing up on a lot of restaurant menus, some of which sprinkle basil leaves on, too, a nice touch, instead of the anchovies. Sometimes, thinly sliced red onion is interleaved among the tomatoes and cheese. Usually no dressing is used, only the olive oil, but a bit of vinaigrette spooned on is good. It should be served only when you can get excellent tomatoes. The quality of the cheese is also very important and if possible, it should be purchased from an Italian grocer who makes it or buys it fresh. The supermarket version, wrapped in plastic, is often hard and flavorless.

Rice Salad
(Preparation time: 5–10 minutes preparing ingredients;
20 minutes cooking rice; 15 minutes chilling)

Serves 4–5

>   1 cup rice
>   2 cloves garlic
>   2 carrots
>   1 green pepper
>   1 red onion
>   6 ozs. fresh green peas (frozen will do)
>   2 large ripe tomatoes
>   3 tbsps. vegetable oil
>   1½ cups chicken broth (canned or made from bouillon powder
>   will do)
>   4 ozs. vinaigrette sauce (see p. 47)

If using frozen peas, allow them to defrost while other work proceeds. Chop garlic fine. Chop carrot fine. If making bouillon from powder, prepare it according to instructions on the label but be careful not to cook for too long or it will become excessively salty. Place oil in a saucepan over high flame. Place chopped garlic in oil. After it begins to brown, add rice and stir until it begins to brown. Add chopped carrot. Add bouillon. While rice and carrots are cooking, chop peppers and onion. Reduce flame to low, cover, simmer over low flame 18 minutes. At this point, rice should be done, but not at all mushy. Remove rice from flame, place in as wide and flat a heat-proof dish as you have. Pour vinaigrette over. Add peppers, onion and peas. Mix thoroughly. Place uncovered in freezer for 15 minutes. Remove. Add tomato and stir together. Refrigerate until ready to serve.

Commentary:

This is our version of a dish which appears in many a French charcuterie.

Frozen corn kernels might be used instead of, or in addition to, the peas. Mixing in bits of poached chicken breast, or cold chopped shrimp turns the salad into a meal.

Salade Chinoise
(Preparation time: 20 minutes)

Serves 4

1 small head of Boston, Bibb or red lettuce
1 cup chopped Chinese cabbage (if unavailable, use more
      lettuce)
1 small bunch watercress
1 red onion
4 qts. water
4 ozs. bean sprouts
4 ozs. fresh mushrooms
4 ozs. water chestnuts
6 ozs. tofu (bean curd)
1 red pepper
Optional: 1 ripe tomato, diced

Dressing:

2 ozs. oil (preferably sesame; if not, peanut)
3 ozs. vinegar (preferably rice)
2 oz. soy sauce
2 tbsps. peanut butter
½ tsp. ginger powder

Wash lettuces, tear Boston, Bibb or red lettuce into bite size pieces. If you can get Chinese cabbage, trim away green leafy part using only the center spine section of each leaf. Cut mushrooms, tofu, water chestnuts, onion and red pepper into slices. Place all salad ingredients in salad bowl. Bring water to boil and discard. Remove bottom half of the bean sprouts. Place bean sprouts in strainer, lower into water for half a minute. Remove, chill under running water. Top salad with bean sprouts. Mix dressing ingredients together until peanut butter dissolves and pour over salad. Toss gently (to avoid breaking up tofu).

Commentary:

Nowadays among the prepared salads one sees at French traiteurs or delicatessens there is almost always a version of this salad, reflecting the recent Southeast Asian immigration to France.

Orange and Onion Salad
(Preparation time: 10 minutes)

Serves 4–6

4 large seedless oranges
1 large sweet onion

Slice onion as thin as you can. Peel and slice oranges. Arrange on a plate alternating orange and onion, each slightly overlapping the other. Spoon vinaigrette dressing over the slices. Serve chilled.

Commentary:

Peaches or tomatoes may be substituted for oranges.

Salad Mei Yan
(Preparation time: 25–30 minutes)

Serves 6

4 celery sticks
4 carrots
1 Chinese cabbage
½ lb. rice noodles
½ lb. tofu (preferably dried)
¼ lb. sliced prosciutto, smithfield or other dried ham
1 cucumber (optional)
½ lb. bean sprouts
2 tbsps. soy sauce
4 ozs. sesame oil
2 ozs. rice vinegar
2 ozs. red rice wine or dry sherry
pot of 2 qts. water

Trim celery, cut each stick into one inch pieces. (Do not slice the celery perpendicular to its length but at an angle of 45 degrees). Appearance is important. Strip the green part away from the Chinese cabbage, leaving the white spine, and slice it into pieces the same length and at the same angle as the celery. Peel, quarter and seed the cucumber (for a fat cucumber, cut in eighths), and slice into pieces the same size and at the same angle as the celery and Chinese cabbage. Shred the carrots on a grater or in a food processor. Remove and discard the bottom half of the bean sprouts. Bring the water to a boil. Place the celery, Chinese cabbage and bean sprouts in a strainer (they may not all fit and so this operation may have to be done more than once). Lower into boiling water for one minute. Place under running cold water and drain. Dry in a spinner or on paper towels.

Boil noodles until cooked *al dente* (firm). Follow timing instruction on label, but test after almost half the time for cooking has passed. If not done, test every minute or two thereafter. When done, place under cold running water.

Cut tofu into slices almost the same size and angle as celery and cabbage.

Cut ham into small pieces, about ½" by 1".

Mix vegetables, noodles, tofu and ham. Add soy, oil, vinegar, wine as dressing. Toss. Chill. Serve.

Commentary:

Salads are not seen often in Chinese restaurants. Mei Yan, who lived with the Greenbergs for two years while attending graduate school often made this salad which we have named after her.

Madame Ariga Salad
(Preparation time: 15 minutes)

½ lb. spinach
¼ lb. fresh mushrooms
2 small cloves garlic
2–3 slices Canadian bacon
¼ cup toasted croutons
3–4 tbsps. vegetable oil
2 tbsps. butter (optional)
3–4 ozs. sauce vinaigrette

Trim spinach leaves, wash thoroughly (after you think all the sand has been removed, wash once more). Dry in spinner or on paper towels. Tear into bite size pieces. Wash and slice mushrooms. Cut garlic cloves into small spear-like slices. Heat oil in pan, sauté garlic until brown. Remove, dry gently on paper towel. Fry bacon until it begins to brown. Remove bacon; cut into small pieces, about ½" by 1."

Use already made croutons (or bread cubes prepared for stuffing) or slice 3–4 slices bread and brown in butter. Mix together spinach, sliced mushrooms, bacon, garlic and croutons. Add vinaigrette.

Commentary:

This basically is a standard spinach salad. What makes it different are the little browned spears of garlic.

We had this version in Tokyo. It was named after Madame Michiko Ariga, the first woman law school graduate in Japan (she is now in her 70s). When she was graduated from law school she could not become a member of the bar—women were not permitted to. She has now become one of that country's foremost experts on trade regulation.

During post-graduate studies in the United States she discovered spinach salad and brought the recipe back to Japan where the chef at the Gen restaurant in Roppongi, Tokyo developed it into this recipe. Since then many people call it Madame Ariga salad. The garlic spears are an important Japanese contribution.

Cordoba Chicken Salad
(Preparation time: 25–30 minutes)

Serves 4–6

   1 lb. chicken breasts
   4 medium red bell peppers
   6 ozs. olive oil
   4½ ozs. vinegar
   salt
   pepper
   2 cloves garlic, sliced
   1 onion
   1 bay leaf

Place chicken breasts in lightly salted boiling water with onion, garlic and bay leaf. Bring to a boil, simmer for 6–10 minutes (depending on thickness) until no longer pink inside. Remove, chill under running water. Cut into ½" strips.

Cut off tops of peppers, remove seeds, slice peppers (including tops) into ½" strips, or (for tops) as close to ½" as possible. Heat

3 ozs. of the oil in a saucepan, add strips and 3 ozs. of the vinegar. Cover, simmer for 15 to 20 minutes. Monitor heat, reducing if necessary to avoid burning.

Remove peppers from pan, place in a large heat proof, flat dish, place in freezer to cool quickly.

Toss peppers and chicken strips.

Mix remaining oil and vinegar and pour over the pepper-chicken mixture.

Refrigerate (or keep in freezer, but do not freeze), then serve.

Commentary:

We had this dish in Cordoba, Spain, where it is a favorite. It is one of ours, too.

SALAD DRESSINGS

Vinaigrette

3 ozs. vegetable or olive oil
1 oz. vinegar
1 clove garlic, finely chopped
1 tsp. Dijon mustard, or ¼ tsp. dry powdered mustard
1 tbsp. chopped fresh herbs if available (or pinch of dried
      rosemary, thyme, tarragon, etc.)
salt
pepper

Commentary:

The above proportions are somewhat arbitrary. Eminent authorities prescribe oil to vinegar ratios ranging from 2 to 1 to more than 5 or 6 to 1. Some use lemon juice in place of or in addition to vinegar which may be of various sorts, e.g. wine, herb, rice, raspberry, etc. Grapefruit juice is quite good. Other oils (peanut, vegetable, walnut) may be substituted. Some gourmets say there isn't a good olive oil available at reasonable prices anymore, and insist on vegetable oil. Others insist olive is a *sine qua non*. A tablespoon or two of chopped shallots, garlic, mustard, pickle, olive and/or lemon peel and chopped egg white might be added as well as capers or chopped onion. Obviously, you don't want to load the sauce with so many chopped ingredients that it looks like an industrial harbor at low tide, but two or three of the foregoing could be very nice. Our only imperative would be: use fresh herbs, if available.

If you don't think it too complicated and productive of more dirty dishes than you can stand, set out dishes of all or most of the potential ingredients so that everyone at the table may mix their own.

Some authorities have written tirades against storing vinaigrette on the ground that its flavor deteriorates and it is so easy to prepare to order. Nevertheless, we find it keeps well refrigerated for a week or longer. Indeed, sometimes we don't even refrigerate it. Since time is of the essence, you might want to make a large quantity at one time.

Aioli (garlic mayonnaise)
(Preparation time: Under 20 minutes)

> **1 large (or equivalent quantity for smaller ones) clove of garlic**
> **1 egg yolk at room temperature**
> **½ tbsp. lemon juice or herb vinegar**
> **1 tbsp. water**
> **½ cup olive oil**
> **salt to taste**

Chop garlic fine, in blender or processor. Add the egg yolk. As the blender or processor blade spins, slowly dribble in the olive oil. About half way through, add the lemon juice or vinegar and water. Add the balance of the oil very slowly until it thickens to look like mayonnaise. Add the salt to taste. If chilled in the refrigerator, it becomes stiffer.

Commentary:

Aioli is Provençal garlic mayonnaise, revered in Southern France.

We have designed this aioli recipe for minimalists, although we prefer more garlic and use it ourselves; but anything in which garlic predominates will be controversial. If you read the experts, you will find the garlic oil ratio for aioli varies (Escoffier: 1 oz. garlic/1 cup oil; Louis P. DeGouy: 2-3 cloves garlic/7-8 or more tbsp. oil; Richard Olney: 3-4 cloves garlic/2 cups oil; Julia Child: 4-8 cloves garlic/1½ cups oil). Since garlic cloves vary considerably in size, there is quite a range among recipes even without other differences. All the authorities make clear, however, that quantities may be adjusted to taste, and moderating ingredients may be added while mixing, e.g., the option of incorporating a slice of crustless (first soaked in milk, water or vinegar) squeezed dry bread or a small boiled potato.

Olney says that the blender impairs the flavor of the olive oil and makes it airy. Child asserts it makes the garlic taste bitter. But, as Olney points out, blender aioli is commonplace in Provence. If one of your objects is speed, we think using the processor or blender instead of the alternative, a mortar and pestle or whisk, is completely justified and that the difference in flavor may not be detectable and surely is not intolerable.

Now, you can shortcut the whole business by squeezing 2 medium-large cloves of garlic into a cup of Hellman's Mayonnaise. Lots of experts couldn't tell the difference.

Aioli is used not only with crudités. It is served with fish (boiled cod), in soups and with vegetables.

Bagna Cauda
(Preparation time: under 20 minutes)

4 ozs. butter
4 ozs. olive oil
1 small tin anchovies (chopped)
2 cloves garlic (finely chopped)
2 tbsps. red wine vinegar

Marinate anchovies in vinegar 5 minutes. Remove from vinegar and place together with other ingredients in a saucepan. Simmer 10 minutes, stirring occasionally. The anchovies should dissolve. Serve and keep hot on a hot tray or over a small warming flame while you dip the vegetables.

Commentary:

Bagna cauda is an Italian dip for vegetables. It also makes a good quick sauce for pasta. As with other sauces, reasonable variations are possible. You might use only butter or olive oil rather than both. Elizabeth David uses equal quantities of all ingredients and notes you may add cream, quantity unspecified. Michael Field is heavier on the olive oil, lighter on the garlic, as is Marcella Hazan, etc. Craig Claiborne adds chopped parsley. Michael Field offers one excellent recipe which substitutes cream for olive oil (2 cups boiled carefully—to avoid burning—until reduced to one) plus the other ingredients and cayenne pepper. Several authors, who wrote in the days before truffle prices became ridiculous, added sliced white truffles.

In dipping vegetables, and carrying from bowl to mouth, one might hold a slice of Italian or French bread under the dripping vegetable to protect tablecloth, necktie, etc. After enough bagna cauda drips onto the bread, eat it.

The vinegar marination of the anchovies is the George Bizos Greek touch which we have used in other recipes.

Cumin Dressing

4 ozs. oil (olive or peanut)
2 ozs. vinegar
1 clove garlic (chopped fine or crushed)
½ tsp. Dijon mustard (or ¼ tsp. mustard powder)
fresh pepper
salt
1½ tsps. cumin seeds

Toast cumin seeds in a pan over medium heat. Crush. Add to other ingredients. (Cumin powder may be used instead).

Commentary:

We have had this dressing at the home of Iphigene Sulzberger whose superb Chilean cook served the salad with paella. It was a perfect match, but it goes well on salads served with or following other dishes.

SALAD GARNISHES

In addition to salad dressings, garnishes of various sorts may flavor and adorn fresh green concoctions. Such fillips are commonplace—even tawdry salad bars offer plastic buckets of bacon bits and bowls of rancid croutons. But garnishes can be tasty, refreshing and attractive looking. Among the more interesting garnishes we have encountered are the following:

Cheese on Onion Slices: Thin onion slices with a melted slice of goat cheese (other cheeses will do) on top, one slice per guest on top of each salad plate, as served: (The combination is too fragile to toss with the salad). We first encountered this garnish, to our delight, at the Ambassade d'Auvergne in Paris. A simple way to make this preparation is to place the onion slices, topped with cheese, in a toaster oven set to broil for 2–3 minutes. (Watch it—all ovens don't function alike).

Nuts: Walnuts sprinkled among the leaves of greens are commonplace, delicious, and served with salad all over Perigord. Try making the salad with walnut oil if you use walnuts. Almonds and pecans go equally well. Toasting in pan shortly before serving enhances flavor.

Sausage: A smattering of thinly sliced sausage is part of some great Chinese salads and goes well with other kinds. Pepperoni is the most readily obtainable sausage which would fit this role. Chinese sausage, if you can get it, is certainly good. Sauté the slices first to make them crisp and melt away the fat.

Cheese: Crumbled blue cheese (Roquefort, Stilton, Gorgon-zola, or unpedigreed bleu or blue adds flavor). Add enough and the dressing becomes a blue cheese dressing.

Croutons: Thin white bread, crust cut away, cut into ½" or 1" squares, browned in butter or butter and garlic are a nice accompaniment.

Bacon Bits: Fry until crisp, then crumble over salad.

Parsley Croutons: Trim white bread slices; in a saucepan brown them in butter. Chop parsley very fine. Mix thoroughly with butter (not the butter you have browned the bread in) to make parsley butter. Butter the browned bread with the parsley butter. Cut into small squares and place on each salad plate as served. Other fresh herbs may be substituted for the parsley.

Anchovies: Soak a tinful in vinegar 5 minutes; toss on the salad.

CHAPTER IV

Simple Soups

Many soups qualify for first course or light meal treatment; others are of the meal-in-itself category. Here we treat simple soups. The next chapter on stews and heavy soups take up the latter.

A glance at the classics would discourage one with ambition to prepare first rate soups quickly. Escoffier prescribes for one type of consomme, the first of his basic soup categories, shin of beef, lean beef, fowls' skeletons, carrots, turnips, leeks, parsnips and onion and four to five hours cooking. Many other serious cookbook authors offer recipes which take a good deal of time to extract the full flavor of meat, bones and vegetables mixing them together by slow simmering and reduction of liquid. The marvelous result cannot be obtained in any other way, but we have imposed upon ourselves a regimen which denies the time for such full treatment. There are various ways to make excellent soups, full of flavor, interest and color in much less time. One technique which we sometimes use to enjoy the best of both the worlds of speedy and authentic cuisine, is to prepare chicken, beef or fish stock from time to time and freeze it in usable portions. Sometimes this may be done by salvaging the broth of poached chicken or fish prepared for another dish (e.g., chicken mole (p. 92) or poached fish (p. 114) and freezing. A simpler procedure, however, is to use canned chicken, beef or clam broth, yogurt, tomato or vegetable juice as the principal medium to carry the other ingredients in the soup. That is the method we usually employ here. Bouillon powder may be used but it is salty and if simmered too long becomes even more so, as liquid evaporates, leaving a higher proportion of salt.

Hot and Sour Broccoli Soup
*(Preparation time: 15 minutes assembling and slicing ingredients;
15 minutes simmering)*

Serves 6–8

32 ozs. chicken broth (preferably canned or from cubes
          or powder)
1 lb. broccoli
4 ozs. pork or beef or chicken
2 ozs. soy sauce
4 ozs. lime juice or rice vinegar
1 oz. dried mushrooms (fresh may be substituted;
          see commentary below)
2 ozs. sliced water chestnuts
¼ tsp. hot sesame oil or if not available, tabasco sauce
1 tsp. fresh grated ginger or ½ tsp. powdered ginger
1 tbsp. cornstarch
12 ozs. water
1 egg

Boil 8 ozs. water and pour over dried mushrooms in a heatproof
bowl. Soak ten minutes. If dried mushrooms have stems, remove
after soaking, as they are too tough to eat. If using fresh mushrooms,
slice and sauté until brown. Slice pork or beef or chicken into very
thin slivers. Slice water chestnuts into ¼" thick slices. Cut broccoli
flowerlets from stems and separate into small units. Slice stem into
very thin slices; keep 4–5 tbsps., discard balance of stems. Bring
broth to a simmer. Add meat, soy sauce, vinegar, water chestnuts,
hot sesame oil (or tabasco), ginger, broccoli. Place corn starch in a
cup, add 4 ozs. cold water, stir to dissolve, add slowly to simmering
bouillon, stirring in. Add mushrooms to bouillon. Beat egg in a
cup and slowly pour into soup, stirring slowly. Allow to simmer
2–3 minutes more. Serve.

Commentary:

This soup is, of course, Chinese in style, but goes well with other main courses. It could be part of a meal of French/Indo-China cuisine. The soy/lime or vinegar ratio may be varied to taste, e.g. 3–1 or 1–3. The amount of hot oil or sauce and/or ginger may be increased if your audience likes food spicy as we do. The egg may be omitted.

Mussel or Clam Soup
(Preparation time: 20–30 minutes or more cleaning and soaking mussels; 5 minutes chopping other ingredients; 10 minutes cooking)

Serves 4–6
>   **30 mussels or clams**
>   **1 large can Italian tomatoes**
>   **1 onion**
>   **2 tbsps. oil**
>   **2 cloves garlic**
>   **1 bay leaf**
>   **1 tsp. oregano**
>   **1 piece orange peel (about ½″ by 2″)**
>   **½ tsp. anise**
>   **5–6 drops tabasco sauce**
>   **2 tbsps. vinegar (optional)**
>   **2 tbsps. flour or cornstarch (optional)**
>   **6–8 ounces dry white wine (optional)**

Scrub mussels or clams, remove mussel "beards" with a small knife. Place in a bowl of cold water. The longer you do this in advance of cooking, the more likely it is that they will be free of sand. The night or morning before serving is not too far in advance, but 20 minutes is better than nothing. 2 tbsps. of vinegar added to the water is said to encourage the mussels to discharge sand. We add the vinegar but have no idea of whether it works. A couple of tablespoons of flour or cornstarch added to the water is said to make the mussels plump. We think it does. Cornstarch, indeed, will encourage the mussels to give up sand. Chop onion, garlic.

Place oil in saucepan, cook onion and garlic gently 5 minutes. Add tomatoes, orange peel and spices. Add white wine, if you use it. Cook over high heat 5–7 minutes. Remove mussels or clams from water. Add to saucepan, cover, keep heat at highest until all mussels or clams open, probably 7–10 minutes. You may with a large spoon, have to move the mussels (or clams) from the bottom of the pan to the top, and vice versa, as those at the bottom open first. Serve.

Commentary:

A hot red pepper may be placed in the tomato broth if you like the dish *picante* (spicy). When the mussels or clams open, they exude a great deal of broth. Serve with warm French or Italian bread. Provide a plate for discarded shells. You will have to wash your hands and face, and perhaps launder clothing after this course.

You could use half mussels and half clams.

Belgian Mussel Soup

Serves 4
  48 mussels
  ½ cup white wine
  1 head celery (leaves and all)
  1 cup water
  1 medium onion, chopped
  6 peppercorns

Scrub mussels and remove "beards" with a small, sharp knife. Place in a bowl of cold water to soak, the longer the better. (See previous recipe regarding soaking.) Cut up the celery into 1" slices. Place the white wine in a saucepan, add the onion, water, and peppercorns. Add half the celery including the leaves. Simmer for 10 minutes. Then extract the leaves with a slotted spoon. (This is for appearance's sake and to make it easier to handle the mussels so it doesn't matter if you miss a few). Add the mussels, cover, raise flame to highest, boil until mussels all open (about 6–7 minutes) moving those on top to the bottom with a spoon so that they get highest heat too. When all are open (there may be a couple of dissidents which will never open—discard them) add the remaining celery and simmer for 2 more minutes. Serve in soup bowls.

Commentary:

Some of the celery will be soft, some crisp, a nice touch.

We first found clams and mussels prepared this way dining around Belgium near Ghent. Having seen "clam chowder" on a menu we ordered it and got the clam-celery soup. The dish is perhaps more widely made with mussels (mosselen). Street vendors sell it maybe as widely as hot dogs are sold in New York.

Avocado Soup
(Preparation time: 5 minutes peeling, slicing avocados;
10 minutes simmering soup)

Serves 4–6

 2 medium size ripe avocados
 2 tbsps. white vinegar
 24 ozs. chicken broth (preferably canned or from powder or
  cubes)
 4 ozs. cream

Remove flesh of one avocado and place in food processor with 1 tbsp. of the vinegar. Add 6 ozs. broth to processor. Cut flesh of other avocado in thin slices and pour remaining vinegar over slices. Place remainder of broth and contents of processor in a saucepan. Bring to simmer. Add cream. Simmer 2 minutes more. Pour into serving bowls and place several of the thin avocado slices on top of soup in each bowl. The flavor of this soup is delicate and consonant with its lovely pale green color.

Mei Yan's Chinese Egg Soup
(Preparation time: 25 minutes)

Serves 4–6

2 eggs
1 tbsp. butter
24 ozs. chicken broth (preferably canned or from powder or
        cubes)
2 ozs. fresh ginger
2 ozs. sherry
½ lb. chicken breasts (or ½ lb. dried ham, e.g. Smithfield or
        prosciutto)
4 large Chinese cabbage leaves
A wok or a small frying pan and a larger saucepan

Slice chicken or ham into narrow strips. Slice ginger into thin, small sticks. Strip green part away from cabbage leaves and discard. Cut remaining white spines into 1″ pieces. If you have a wok, melt butter in it, beat eggs and fry them in the wok. If you don't have a wok, fry the beaten eggs in the butter in a frying pan and gently slide into saucepan. Place the wok or saucepan over medium flame and gently pour the broth in beside the fried egg. It will float to the top of the broth. Add sherry. As the broth simmers, tuck neatly under the egg the chicken or ham, cabbage and ginger. Simmer gently for twenty minutes. Serve from wok or pot, serving each guest a share of the soup with a segment of the fried egg.

Commentary:

First of all this dish is unlike anything we have seen in any Chinese restaurant. It also tastes first rate. Mei Yan, our Chinese friend, has prepared it for us.

If you use bouillon powder or cubes the soup may become too salty as the volume reduces. If so, add a bit of boiling water before serving.

Asparagus Soup
(Preparation time: 25 minutes)

Serves 4–6

> ½ lb. asparagus
> 24 ozs. chicken broth
> 4 ozs. ham (preferably Smithfield or prosciutto or similar
>   dried ham)
> 2 ozs. cream
> ¼ tsp. nutmeg

Cut away tough ends of asparagus and discard. Cut off the tops of half of the asparagus and set aside. Cut ham into thin strips. Simmer asparagus (but not the removed tips) in chicken broth ten minutes. Remove asparagus from broth. Place the asparagus (other than the reserved tips) and 6 ozs. of the broth in a food processor and liquify. Return to the saucepan. Add the reserved tips, the ham and cream. Simmer 2–3 minutes, add nutmeg, serve.

Commentary:

You may, if you prefer, omit the cream. The soup may be served cold. For this, chill in freezer. But if served cold, it is better with cream.

Pea Soup/Broccoli Soup/Cauliflower Soup
*(Preparation time: 10 minutes shelling peas, if fresh;
10 minutes cooking)*

Serves 4–6

For Pea Soup (see *Commentary* to adapt for Broccoli or
Cauliflower Soup):

**24 ozs. chicken broth (preferably canned or from cubes or
           powder)**
1 lb. fresh or 12 ozs. frozen green peas
6 ozs. heavy cream
2 tsps. curry powder
½ tsp. ground white pepper

Place half the peas and 6 ozs. of the broth in a food processor
or blender and liquify them. Place remainder of broth and liquified
peas in a saucepan, bring to simmer, add remainder of peas, curry
powder, pepper and cream. Return to simmer. If using fresh peas,
simmer 5 minutes. If frozen, simmer 2–3 minutes. Serve.

Commentary:

More peas (puréed and/or whole) make soup richer. Other
vegetables, e.g. broccoli, cauliflower may be used the same way.
Cut 1 head of broccoli or cauliflower into tiny flowerlets. Slice the
stems into a cupful of thin slices. Purée half of the slices along with
6 ozs. of the broth in blender or processor. Simmer the remainder
and the flowerlets for 4 to 5 minutes. Curry powder should be used
with cauliflower. Add 1 tbsp. of finely chopped red pepper for
color. With broccoli we use ½ tsp. nutmeg instead of curry powder.

These soups may be served cold; simply place in freezer until
chilled.

Gazpacho

(Preparation time: 20⁺ minutes chopping vegetables and sautéing mushrooms, 3–4 minutes mixing; 20 minutes chilling)

Serves 6–8

2 cloves garlic
⅓ cup sliced mushrooms (canned sliced mushrooms may be
      substituted)
3 tbsps. olive oil
1 cup finely chopped onions
2 cups finely chopped tomatoes (canned should be used during
      those seasons when they are superior to fresh)
1¼ cups green pepper chopped (red and hard to find yellow
      peppers may be mixed with the green)
1 cup finely chopped cucumber (preferably peeled and
      seeded)
2 tsps. chives
1 tbsp. chopped parsley (if available, other chopped fresh
      garden herbs as well)
½ tsp. tabasco
1 tsp. Worcestershire sauce
½ cup tarragon vinegar
3 cups tomato or vegetable juice
2 tsps. salt
1 tsp. freshly ground black pepper

Optional: Garlic croutons

3–4 slices white bread
2 cloves garlic
2 tbsps. olive or other oil or butter

Chop ingredients; crush garlic in 1 tsp. salt. Sauté mushrooms 4–5 minutes in olive oil over high heat. Combine all ingredients in a wide steel or glass bowl. Place in freezer 20 minutes or more to chill. Be careful not to freeze.

Garlic croutons: You may sprinkle garlic croutons on each soup bowl. Croutons are made by trimming crusts from (preferably white) bread slices, cut into 1″ squares. Chop garlic fine. Sauté garlic 2–3 minutes over medium heat. Place bread in pan with garlic. Stir and turn until browned on both sides. Prefabricated croutons sold for poultry stuffing are a time saver.

Commentary:

Gazpacho is essentially a salad in liquid form. You have a bit of a head start if the tomato or vegetable juice has been refrigerated first. If you start with the tomato and tomato juice base, any fresh, available vegetables appropriately may be added. Some prefer gazpacho without onions. Some don't like the hot sauce. We like both. Zucchini may be added or substituted for cucumbers; finely chopped carrot or celery work well; fresh (or frozen) corn kernels or peas go well also. A more viscous version is made with canned tomatoes instead of tomato juice, whirled once or twice in a food processor, or mashed thoroughly with a fork. See what's available in the garden or at the greengrocer, gauge your audience and perform accordingly.

Gazpacho Clam Soup
(Preparation time: 20⁺ minutes chopping vegetables, sautéing mushrooms, 3–4 minutes mixing ingredients; 15–20 minutes scrubbing and cooking clams; 10 minutes chilling)

Same ingredients and procedure as for gazpacho but only half as much tomato or vegetable juice
2 doz. cherrystone clams (other clams will do)

Prepare other ingredients as for gazpacho. Place in freezer. Scrub clams. Place in cold water until ready to proceed further. The longer they are in the water, the more likely they are to be free of sand. Some say adding a bit of vinegar improves the sand shedding process. Place clams in a saucepan. Cover. Turn heat to high. When clams are open (cook at least 6–7 minutes) place pan, containing clams and broth in freezer until cool, about 10 minutes. Remove clams from shells, cut in half or quarters if they are large. Add clams and broth (being careful not to pour off sand, if any, into soup) to gazpacho. Serve.

Tomato Dill Soup/Broccoli Soup/Spinach Soup
(Preparation time: 5 minutes chopping, 15 minutes simmering; 15–20 minutes in freezer, chilling)

Serves 4–6

> **24 ozs. chicken broth**
> **3 large tomatoes (or equivalent volume of canned tomatoes)**
> **1 small clove garlic (chopped fine or pressed in a garlic press)**
> **¼ tsp. ground pepper**
> **1 tbsp. tomato paste**
> **¾ cup cream**
> **1 medium onion sliced**
> **1 tsp. salt**
> **¼ cup water**
> **¼ tsp. chopped dill (preferably fresh, dried will do)**

Slice fresh tomatoes if you are using them. Add all ingredients to a saucepan and cover. Simmer 10 minutes. Put in blender or food processor and process until smooth. Chill 15–20 minutes in freezer before serving.

Commentary:

These chilled soups—and many other cold vegetable soups which you can develop on your own—add flavor and elegance out of proportion to limited effort. While fresh dill is a strong plus if it is available, our feeling is that what is lost by using dried dill should not discourage you. This soup may be made with spinach or broccoli; in such case omit dill and substitute ¼ tsp. nutmeg and ¼ tsp. cinnamon.

Cucumber Soup
*(Preparation time: 10 minutes chopping, trimming vegetables,
20–25 minutes cooking; 15 minutes in freezer)*

Serves 6–8

    2 tbsps. butter
    ¼ cup chopped shallots (or onion)
    2 cucumbers
    1 tsp. wine vinegar
    ½ tsp. dill (fresh or dried)
    4 cups chicken broth
    3 tbsps. quick cooking farina
    ½ cup sour cream

Chop shallots or onion; peel cucumbers, quarter, cut away and
discard seeds, cut into 1″ chunks.

Melt butter in 3 qt. saucepan, sauté shallots or onion 1 minute.
Add chicken broth, cucumbers, vinegar, dill. Bring to boil. Add
farina. Simmer 20 minutes uncovered or until farina is tender.
Puree in blender or food processor. May be served hot or cold. If
cold, chill 15 minutes in freezer in as shallow a pan as will hold
the soup and refrigerate until ready to serve. Add sour cream and
stir in just before serving.

Cucumber Yogurt Soup
(Preparation time: 10–15 minutes, trimming, chopping)

Serves 4–6

    3 cups plain yogurt
    2 cloves garlic
    1 bunch scallions (1 medium onion may be substituted)
    1 large cucumber
    2 tbsps. vinegar
    1 tbsp. chopped fresh dill (dried may be substituted)
    ½ tsp. cayenne pepper (optional)
    salt to taste

Peel and quarter cucumber, scoop out seeds. Chop garlic, scallions and dill fine. Place half of the cucumber and half of the scallions (equal proportions of white and green parts) in a food processor or blender. Blend together for 10 seconds. Pour into serving bowl. Chop balance of cucumber coarsely. Stir in remaining ingredients. Chill until ready to serve.

Commentary:

This soup may be made with fresh zucchini or with spinach or tiny flowerlets of broccoli or cauliflower which first have been simmered in salt water for 2–3 minutes and chilled under running water before adding to the yogurt. As with the cucumber, half of the vegetables should be blended with the yogurt—the other half chopped and added to the mixture. In any of these soups, most fresh herbs other than dill may be used.

Onion Soup
(Preparation time: 5–7 minutes slicing, crushing garlic; 10⁺ minutes sautéing; 20 minutes simmering; 5–10 minutes baking)

Serves 4–6

3 cups thin-sliced yellow onion (Bermuda or red will do)
4 tbsps. butter
1½ qts. strong beef broth. (If you make the soup from beef
       bouillon cubes or powder, use 1½ times the amount
       of cubes or powder recommended on the label)
1 clove garlic
freshly ground pepper
2 tsp. sugar
1 tbsp. flour
3 tbsps. brandy
¼ cup dry sherry or dry white wine
¾ cup grated parmesan cheese (romano, asiago, swiss or
       jarlsberg are acceptable)
4–6 slices toasted French bread

Preheat oven to 450 degrees. In large pot melt butter and add sliced onions. Sauté onions about 10 minutes or longer over medium flame until they are soft, translucent and golden. Add crushed garlic and sugar, stir and then dust flour over onions and stir again. Sauté additional two minutes. If onions are not yet light brown, sauté several minutes more until they are. Add the stock and grind in fresh pepper to taste. (If using bouillon cubes or powder, do not add salt before tasting, after soup is finished, as the bouillon is very salty and no additional salt may be necessary—indeed you may have to add a bit of boiling water to reduce salinity.) Simmer 10 minutes.

Divide soup among four-six oven-proof individual dishes or crocks and spread half the grated cheese over these. Wet one side of the toasted French bread in the soup and place a piece of the toast on the top of each bowl wet side up; sprinkle the remaining cheese over the pieces of toast. Place the bowls in the oven and bake 5–10 minutes or until cheese is lightly browned.

(If you do not have individual oven-proof bowls, you can put the soup in a single large bowl, float the toast and cheese on the top and bake as above.)

Commentary:

Assuming you use a purchased beef broth (or your own, previously made), this soup can be prepared in well under an hour. Since much of the time is cooking time, you will have ample opportunity to do other things. It is rich and filling—a fair sized meal in itself, if topped off with a light salad and/or fruit. If you should plan to serve onion soup as a first course before a main meat dish, you can produce a lighter, less filling dish by eliminating the flour and the toast and cutting back on the cheese.

Spinach Soup
(Preparation time: 5 minutes washing, trimming spinach;
3–4 minutes grinding spices and beating eggs;
10 minutes simmering soup)

Serves 4–6

24 ozs. chicken broth
½ lb. spinach
1 tsp. cumin
1 tsp. coriander
½ tsp. anise
1 egg

Wash spinach 3–5 times to remove sand. When you think it is free of sand wash once more. Tear off and discard stems. Grind spices together. Break egg and beat lightly in a cup. Bring broth to a simmer. Add spices. Add spinach. Simmer 8–9 minutes. Slowly drip egg into soup and stir. Serve.

Commentary:

A nifty way of adding the egg is to pour it into a strainer over the soup while it simmers. Slowly circle the strainer above the saucepan. The egg will come down in streams, forming strings in the soup as it reaches the hot liquid and hardens.

CHAPTER V

Eight Stews (or Meal Sized Soups)

Gumbo; Chili con carne;
Bouillabaisse type fish stew;
Borscht; Lamb pilaf; Choucroute;
Mozambican rice; Linguica Stew

Most of these stews are based on a regional or national special-ty, the proper composition of which stirs strident controversy. With each you can go a long way beyond classically prescribed in-gredients and procedures before you are out of bounds. We go so far beyond bouillabaisse, however, that we wonder whether our prescription deserves that title and, therefore, have hedged by naming it bouillabaisse type. Of course, we do not use the quintes-sential rascasse or other Mediterranean fish; to save time, our broth is based on bottled clam juice, and is not extracted from bones and heads. Heretically, (for bouillabaisse, but not some other fish stews) we add white wine to the broth, perhaps to as-suage guilt inflicted by other deficiencies, possibly only because we savor the flavor. We are consoled, by knowing that other regional fish stews depart from bouillabaisse in all sorts of particulars. Ours, we fantasize, might have been invented and relished on the beach of some lost Atlantic or Mediterranean cove, but never recorded.

As to gumbo, our great omission is the roux. But it takes at least 10 minutes to prepare. Some will insist that without that base of browned-flour-simmered-in-fat the color, flavor and consistency of gumbo are unattainable. Perhaps, but Craig Claiborne's *New York Times Cookbook* omits the roux, while his *Favorites* pre-scribes it, simmered for 20–40 minutes "or longer"! And *he* hails from Louisiana! James Beard omits roux, as does the Grand Central Oyster Bar. Yet Lillian Hellman's gumbo, our favorite, starts with a roux. The clincher for us was not only time, but that K-Paul's a widely acclaimed New Orleans restaurant, although controversial among long time New Orleans residents, leaves out the roux. Our mission, excellence within time constraints, causes us to come down on the side of the non-roux types.

Chili con carne is a sort of Dagwood sandwich of stews, a sometimes mindless, protean concoction, composed within the broadest limits. It demands only chili powder, or some equivalent thereof (dried chilies if you are ambitious, but too time consuming for this book), ground or cubed meat (beef, pork or even chicken will do—we once had Buffalo meat chili in Laramie, Wyoming—it was terrible), perhaps kidney beans (another causa belli), perhaps some tomatoes and/or other vegetables and the pugnacity to defend your creation. Some think chili con carne must be chili con carne con frijoles (with beans), but others use rice, not beans. We prefer it with neither.

Borscht may be the "meal in itself" dish, but also, if less meat were used, could be served as a soup.

Gumbo
(Preparation time: 30–40 minutes)

Serves 4–6

4 strips bacon
1 lb. okra (fresh, frozen or canned); if fresh, trimmed and
     sliced in 1″–2″ segments
2 green peppers, chopped
2 medium onions, chopped
1 large can tomatoes
2 large cloves garlic, chopped
6 ozs. chorizo, pepperoni, or breakfast sausage sliced thin
2 bottles clam juice
2 tbsps. Worcestershire
2 bay leaves
1 tsp. oregano
¼ tsp. ground nutmeg
¼ tsp. ground cloves
salt, pepper to taste
2 tbsps. gumbo file (important but optional)
tabasco

The meat and/or seafood: All or any combination of the following may be added:

Boneless chicken breasts cut into 1" strips
Sausage (Chorizo, pepperoni or breakfast sausage)
Shrimp
Oysters
Crabmeat

Quantities should be adjusted to allow 8 ounces per person. In other words, for 4–6 persons there should be 32–48 ounces of meat and/or seafood altogether.

2 cups rice

Place 2 cups rice in saucepan. Add 4 cups water. Simmer 18–20 minutes or until all water is absorbed. While rice is cooking make the gumbo, as follows:

Cut the bacon into ½"–1" pieces. Cook over medium flame in large pot. When fat has melted, place onions and garlic in pot and sauté about 5–6 minutes over medium flame until soft. If bacon does not provide enough fat to sauté onions and garlic add 2 tbsps. vegetable oil. Add okra, green pepper, tomatoes, spices, clam juice.

If using sausage, brown in a separate pan; pour off fat. Add to large pot.

If using chicken, add to pot at this point. Simmer, pot lid slightly ajar, 20 minutes. If you are using canned okra the time could be 5 minutes less, as it has been cooked in the canning process.

If you are using shrimp you may shell it during the simmering or after serving. Add shrimp. Allow gumbo to return to a boil and simmer for 3–4 minutes. At this point, you may simmer perhaps up to an hour longer, if you are not ready to serve. Keep stirring to avoid burning.

If you are using oysters, add them to simmering gumbo, about 5 minutes before serving, allow to return to boil and immediately remove from flame.

If you are using crabmeat, remove gumbo from flame and while quite hot sprinkle crabmeat on top.

While quite hot add gumbo file, if you can get it, and stir in thoroughly.

Serve with tabasco bottle at table.

Commentary:

The gumbo file (ground dried sassafras leaves) imparts flavor and color and thickens the preparation too, but may not be readily available. The concoction can be excellent without it.

Chili con Carne
(Preparation time: 50 minutes)

Serves 4–6

   2 lbs. hamburger meat
   8 ozs. canned chicken broth (or broth made from cubes or
            powder)
   1 green pepper
   2 onions
   4 cloves garlic
   2 carrots
   2 sticks celery
   2 medium tomatoes
   2 tbsps. chili powder
   2 ozs. unsweetened chocolate
   1 tsp. curry powder
   2 bay leaves
   ½ tsp. ground nutmeg
   ¼ tsp. ground cloves
   salt
   pepper
   4 tbsps. cooking oil
   1 can cooked red kidney beans or
   1 cup rice, cooked according to directions on package

Garnish:

   1 chopped medium onion
   8 ozs. ground parmesan or other hard cheese grated
            (e.g., romano, asiago) or cheddar
   tabasco or chopped hot green pepper, e.g. chilies, serranos
            or jalapeños
   1 pt. sour cream (optional)

Chop onions and garlic. In a large pot, sauté 2 onions and garlic 5–6 minutes in the oil over medium flame until soft. Chop pepper and slice carrots thin, add to pot. In a separate pan brown ground meat. Pour off fat and liquid and add meat to kettle. Chop tomatoes and add to pot. Add chicken broth, chocolate, chili powder, curry powder, bay leaves, nutmeg, cloves, salt, ground pepper to taste. Simmer covered 30 minutes. Chop and add celery and simmer 10 minutes more.

Rinse and drain canned kidney beans, if you are using them. If you are using rice, boil according to instructions on box (usually twice the volume of water as rice, simmer for 18–20 minutes or until all water is absorbed) while chili is cooking. Place 2–3 heaping tbsps. of beans or rice on each platter and pour chili over. Top with chopped raw onion, ground cheese, sour cream and/or hot peppers or tabasco to taste.

Commentary:

There may be thousands of chili recipes and annual contests regularly bring new ones to light. But variations don't go terribly far afield. Pork or beef (or buffalo or venison) or combinations of meat may be cut into small cubes rather than ground, then browned before adding to stew. Actually, cubed meat in chili tastes pretty good but takes a bit more cooking time. Try the little chunks instead of ground meat if you're not in a hurry. Chicken, if it is all you have, or leftover chicken (or indeed leftover anything) is useable. Chili powders vary and you will have to be satisfied with what you find unless you want to make your own, which is not hard. Dried chilies anchos may be the basis of a home made chili powder to which, to taste, one might add a small chili pequin and/or pasilla and/or serrano. These can be quite piquant or picante, or hot, so be careful. All may be found in stores which specialize in Mexican foods. A pinch of cumin seeds, mace and/or turmeric might be added. We have tried to accommodate a striving for individuality with economy of time by using curry powder. But since chili con carne is a highly individualistic preparation you have a lot of scope.

Bouillabaisse Style Fish Stew
(Preparation time: 5 minutes chopping; 30–35 minutes cooking)

Serves 4–6

8 ozs. fish and shellfish per person, i.e. 32–48 ozs. fish and
shellfish combined. The fish may include sole, cod,
bluefish, monkfish, or anything else in the market.
The fish will be easier to use if filleted. Shellfish may
include shrimp, clams, mussels. Cut up fish filets
into bite size pieces.

24 ozs. clam juice
8 ozs. white wine
4 ozs. olive oil
2 onions
4 cloves garlic
1 slice orange peel
2 tomatoes
1 tsp. dried fennel seeds or 2 pieces (2"–3" x 2"–3")
fresh fennel
2 bay leaves
2–3 sprigs fresh parsley
1–2 pinches saffron (optional)
salt
6 black peppercorns

Garlic bread:

1 loaf French bread
4 tsps. garlic
2 tbsps. oil or butter

Rouille: See below

Scrub shellfish and place in cold water. Slice onion, crush
garlic, simmer in the olive oil, 5–6 minutes. When onions are limp,
add clam juice, wine and all ingredients other than fish and seafood.

Simmer 25 minutes. Strain and discard solid material. Reserve the strained liquid, place in saucepan, bring to boil, add fish and shellfish. When liquid simmers again, keep at simmer until shellfish open. Move them around with a spoon so that all receive heat. Be careful not to break up fish.

Serve over a slice of garlic bread placed in each bowl. To make garlic bread, chop garlic cloves fine, sauté in butter or oil for 3–4 minutes, divide garlic and oil or melted butter over each slice.

You may add rouille to enjoy its special flavor and make the stew more picante. We find it hard to eat the fish stew without it. The rouille can be made while the broth is simmering.

Rouille (optional but highly recommended):

1 boiled potato or 2 slices white bread
1 pimento
2 cloves garlic
2–3 ozs. olive oil
Tabasco

The boiled potato is cooked in the soup liquid while it simmers. If using bread soak in a few ounces of soup liquid. Pimento from a can or jar will do, or you might follow the pimento and anchovy recipe to prepare one fresh, if there is time. Crush garlic in a garlic crusher or mince very fine, mash potato, or soaked bread, mash pimento, add to blender or food processor with enough (a few tbsps.) soup broth so blade can mix ingredients. Slowly dribble in olive oil until mixture attains a thick, slushy consistency. Add a few drops of tabasco. The taste should be quite picante. Each diner adds rouille to stew to taste.

Beef Borscht

(Preparation time: 10–15 minutes preparation, trimming, chopping; 30–40 minutes cooking)

Serves 6–8

2 lbs. stew beef
2 qts. water

All of the following vegetables should be shredded or chopped:

2 cups raw beets
1 cup turnips
1 large or 2 medium onion(s)
1 small or ½ large cabbage, preferably green
1 stalk celery
1 cup carrots
½ cup tomato puree
3 tbsps. white vinegar
1 tbsp. sugar
1 tsp. pepper
2 tsps. salt
8 ozs. sour cream

Trim beef and cut into ¼" or smaller cubes. Place in pot. Add onions to pot. Shred or chop beets, turnips, carrots, celery, onions and cabbage; reserve the cabbage and a few tablespoons of beets, turnips, carrots and celery. Add the vegetables (not those reserved), tomato purée, vinegar and sugar to pot. Add water. Boil lightly with lid on for 30 minutes, checking after 25 minutes to make sure water has not largely evaporated. Add shredded cabbage and reserved shredded vegetables. Taste and season further with salt and pepper, if necessary.

Spoon the sour cream on individual servings to taste.

Commentary:

A standard recipe from which this one is adapted takes an hour and a half. We cut the time at no perceptible loss in flavor by cutting the beef into small pieces, instead of using large chunks, by boiling vigorously instead of simmering. The uncooked vegetables added at the end are a fresh, crunchy counterpoint to the other ingredients which have been cooked until quite soft. The result concedes nothing to traditional recipes. Yogurt may be substituted for the sour cream.

Quick Choucroute
(Preparation time: 45 minutes)

Serves 6–8

2 16 ozs. jars of sweet and sour cabbage
6 sausages (preferably German) of different sorts or chunks
    of larger sausages (e.g., knockwurst, bratwurst,
    weisswurst)
½ lb. chicken breasts cut into strips
¼ lb. bacon
3 pork chops or equivalent amount of smoked pork, if you
    can find it
2 ozs. gin
4 ozs. white wine
2 tbsps. caraway seeds
pepper

Cut bacon strips into 3 or 4 pieces. In a large pan cook bacon until soft. Puncture sausage skins in 5 or 6 places with a fork. Add cabbage, gin, wine, caraway seeds, sausages, pork chops. Cover and simmer for 35 minutes.

Commentary:

The Greenbergs first savored this great Alsatian dish in Strasbourg, seat of the European Commission of Human Rights. Some day the area will be more widely known for the Commission than for the choucroute, but perhaps that has not yet occurred. Our version uses the sweet and sour cabbage rather than sauerkraut, but surely sauerkraut—the ingredient of the original—may be used. The gin is an easy substitute for not widely available juniper berries. Other meats may be used instead of or in addition to those prescribed.

Loraine Chaskalson's Lamb Pilaf
(Ground lamb with herbs, nuts, raisins)

(Preparation time: 40 minutes)

Serves 4–6

    2 lbs. ground lamb
    16 ozs. chicken broth
    2 large cloves garlic
    6 tbsps. olive oil
    1 cup tomato puree or canned tomatoes
    4 ozs. raisins
    18 pitted olives (may be stuffed with pimento) cut in halves
    18 almonds roughly chopped
    2 bay leaves
    1 tsp. oregano
    ½ tsp. nutmeg
    ¼ tsp. cinnamon
    ½ tsp. allspice
    salt to taste
    pepper to taste
    medium onion (chopped)
    1 cup rice
    1 cup yogurt or sour cream (optional)

Rice

Over medium flame brown the chopped onion in 3 tbsps. of the olive oil. Add the rice and stir 3–4 minutes until it is coated with the oil. Add 2 cups chicken broth or two cups boiling water and 2 tbsps. chicken bouillon powder. Place on medium to low flame and simmer 18–20 minutes covered, or until water is absorbed. Rice is not all the same and may take less time or longer. The instructions on the box should be your best guide to timing.

Lamb

While rice is cooking, in a large skillet heat the other 3 tbsps. of the olive oil, chop and add the garlic. As garlic browns—over medium flame—add the ground lamb. Raise flame to high and stir until lamb is all browned. Remove skillet from flame and pour off fat. Return to medium flame, add tomato puree or tomatoes, raisins, and spices. Stir as mixture cooks three or four minutes. Add almonds and olives and serve over the rice.

Several tablespoons of yogurt or sour cream may be spooned over each portion.

Commentary:

Arthur and Loraine Chaskalson serve this dish at large parties, often for defendants in political cases, at their home in Johannesburg. Arthur is one of the leading lawyers in South Africa, practicing what we would call civil rights law and Loraine teaches English literature at the University of the Witswatersrand. The origin of the dish is apparently middle Eastern, but curiously, we haven't seen it anywhere in the middle East—which doesn't mean it doesn't exist there.

Mozambican Rice
(Preparation time: 20 minutes)

Serves 6

Left-over spicy rice
Left-over meat or chicken, preferably well-flavored
1 box shelled peas (frozen will do)
1 sweet red pepper
1 carrot
2 medium onions, sliced
2 large cloves garlic
bunch coriander leaves, chopped
1 tsp. fresh ginger, chopped
2 ozs. cooking oil
2 ozs. soy sauce (to taste)
1 tsp. cayenne pepper (or more to taste)
assorted fruit peeled and sliced
3 hard-boiled eggs sliced

Brown the onions, stir in garlic, ginger and cayenne, add the chopped-up meat or chicken and coriander leaves, pour on soy sauce, stir for 2 minutes, add the rice (about half at a time) and stir-fry actively until the rice is hot and evenly light brown.

Place on large serving dish (can be a tray with foil), decorate vigorously and serve still hot.

Commentary:

Albie Sachs invented this dish in his apartment in Maputo, Mozambique, based on his memory of dishes prepared by a former P.O.W. in Indonesia.

He advises: The secret is to ensure that the rice is spiced-up with sticks, leaves and seeds when it is drying out. Cardoman seeds and a little cumin are especially good. The rice and meat can be prepared the night before and cooked up after the guests arrive. Spectacular decoration helps.

Albie Sachs is a South African who left the country after having been imprisoned for anti-apartheid activities. He then taught law in England and Mozambique and has lectured at Columbia and Harvard. *The Jail Diary of Albie Sachs* is an important memoir which has been made into a stage and television play by the Royal Shakespeare Company. In 1988, a bomb which had been placed in his car in Maputo, blew up, causing him to lose an arm and partial sight in one eye. He left Mozambique for London and shortly after reviewing this recipe with us in London in Spring 1990, he returned to South Africa.

Linguica Stew
(Preparation time: 15 minutes; 20 minutes cooking time)

Serves 4

1 lb. linguica (Portuguese) sausage
1 medium onion, sliced
1 medium can red kidney beans
1 navel orange, sliced
1 oz. bourbon
1 small or ½ large cabbage, cut in chunks
Tabasco to taste

Brown linguica and onions. Add beans, bourbon and orange. Cook 5–10 minutes. Add water to arrive at desired consistency, a little sludgy. Bring to boil, add cabbage for 5 minutes longer. Add Tabasco to taste.

Note: If you have time to make this ahead, you can cool for a while, then skim off the fat. Cabbage can be cooked during the first or second stage.

Commentary:

This recipe was perfected by Mike Sviridoff, former vice president of the Ford Foundation and a friend of all of ours, who spends as much time as he can on Martha's Vineyard. Portuguese cookery is an important part of Vineyard cuisine.

CHAPTER VI

Main Meat Dishes

Some of our main meat dishes may be found in the stew chapter and some may be used as main dishes or appetizers. Others are set forth here. We omit the simple grilled steak or chop, assuming that they are self evident or can be found in many other cookbooks.

BEEF

Steak au Poivre
(Preparation time: 15 minutes)

Serves 4

4 ½–¾ lb. sirloin steaks, preferably at least ½" thick
⅛ pound butter
3 tbsps. cognac, sherry or scotch
2 tbsps. lemon juice
1 tbsp. Worcestershire sauce
chopped parsley
freshly ground black pepper, to taste
salt

Rub pepper into both sides of steaks by hand. Sprinkle salt in skillet, bring to high heat and add steaks. Do each side for a minute at high heat and then cook to taste. 1½–2 minutes each side for ½" steak will produce a rare steak. Put half of butter, lemon, Worcestershire on each side while cooking. Add liquor. If you use Cognac or Scotch, flame it—carefully. Spoon sauce from pan onto steak.
Sprinkle with parsley before serving.

Commentary:

Steak au Poivre is an example of how a few minutes preparation can add a special quality to a familiar meat course. However, it must be noted that for many people a good steak with nothing added but salt and pepper is such a treat and sufficiently unusual that they will not want to mess around with any elaboration. If you feel like that, you may want to reserve this recipe for steaks that you have reason to believe are a little less than the best, although here, as with most every dish, the better the components, the better the final product.

We have found that most current recipes for Steak au Poivre are so spicy that they border on the painful and make the flavor of the steak and other ingredients almost irrelevant. That is of course a matter of taste, but if you are cooking for more than one person and are not sure that everyone likes lots of pepper, it may be wise to adhere to our low-voltage spice level and let people add a bit more pepper at the table if they wish.

Beef Stroganoff
(Preparation time: 35 minutes)

Serves 4–5

-

    1½ lbs. filet of beef, cut in thin strips
    1 medium size onion, chopped very fine
    ½–1 lb. fresh mushrooms, wiped with a damp cloth and
           sliced thin
    ½ lb. butter
    1 pt. sour cream
    1 tbsp. Italian tomato paste
    juice of ¼ lemon
    1 tsp. salt
    ¼ tsp. pepper
    ½ tsp. paprika

Heat ⅓ of the butter in a skillet over a full flame until golden brown. Add half of the meat and brown on all sides. Transfer to a large shallow casserole. Add another ⅓ of the butter to the skillet and brown the rest of the meat. Add to casserole. Brown the onion and mushrooms in the balance of the butter. Stir in the tomato paste and paprika. Mix in the sour cream and pour over the meat in the casserole. Cover and simmer in a medium oven (350 degrees) for 20 minutes. Add lemon juice, salt and pepper and stir well. The meat is juicier if seasoned at the end.

Steak Tandoori Style
(Preparation time: 25 minutes; 11–13 minutes broiling time)

2 lbs. flank steak (other cuts are also suitable)
4 ozs. lime juice
1 tsp. cayenne pepper
2 large cloves garlic
1 onion
4 ozs. yogurt
1 medium or 2 small tomatoes (canned or fresh)
salt

Make a dozen small holes in both sides of steak with point of a knife. Crush garlic, rub into steak with cayenne pepper and salt. Add lime juice. Allow to marinate at room temperature 20 minutes, turning over once or twice.

Preheat broiler very hot.

Chop onion and tomato. Mix with yogurt.

Dry steak with paper towel. Cover one side of steak with half the yogurt-onion-tomato mixture. Place in broiler yogurt side up for 6 or 7 minutes for flank steak (medium rare). For other steaks add one or two minutes to regular broiling time (determined by thickness and how rare or done you like it: the yogurt somewhat insulates the steak from the heat). Turn over. Spread yogurt on second side. Broil additional 5 or 6 minutes for flank steak, or a bit longer (allowing time for the yogurt insulation) for other steaks. The yogurt coating should be slightly flecked with burnt crust when done.

Quick Beef Bourguignon
(Preparation time: 10 minutes preparation; 40 minutes cooking time)

Serves 4–6

2 lbs. chuck steak (other beef will do)
½ lb. small (ping pong ball size) white onions (or similarly
   sized pieces of larger onions)
2 carrots
6 small potatoes (ping pong ball size or similarly small pieces
   of larger potatoes)
1 cup red wine
6 tbsps. cooking oil
2 cloves garlic
2 bay leaves
1 tsp. mixed dried herbs (e.g. oregano, marjoram, thyme)
1 dozen dried mushrooms

Boil 2 cups water; soak dried mushrooms in it. Cut steak into
no larger than ½" cubes. Slice garlic, peel onions, peel carrots and
cut into 1" pieces. Place oil in saucepan, brown garlic in it, brown
pieces of meat in it. Add potatoes, onions, carrots, bay leaves,
herbs and wine. Cut stems from mushrooms and discard. Quarter
mushrooms and add to pot. Strain sand, if any from water in which
mushrooms soaked and add to pot. Cover, simmer for 40 minutes
with pot lid slightly open to allow vapor to escape and liquid to
reduce.

Chinese Beef and Vegetables
(Preparation time: 15 minutes preparation; 10 minutes cooking time)

Serves 4–6

2 lbs flank steak
2 large ripe tomatoes
2 medium onions
1 green pepper
4 tbsps. peanut or vegetable oil
2 cloves garlic
½ cup canned water chestnuts
½ cup bean sprouts
1 tsp. chopped ginger
1 tsp. sugar
2 ozs. sherry

Slice steak in ⅛″ slices. If steak is wide make slices no longer than 2‴'s. Cut tomatoes into eighths. Cut onions into eighths. Mince garlic. Slice water chestnuts into ⅛″ slices. Seed green pepper and cut into ½″ slices. Place oil in pan, heat, add garlic and ginger, cook until garlic is brown. Add onion and pepper, sauté over low flame 5 minutes. Remove garlic, onion and pepper and set aside. Add meat to pan, raise heat high. Stir as meat browns. Add soy sauce, sherry and sugar, tomato and water chestnuts. Stir for 1 minute. Return pepper and onion to pan. Heat all ingredients together for 1 minute. Serve.

Meatloaf
(Preparation time: 10 minutes preparation; 35 minutes cooking time)

> 2 lbs. ground beef
> 2 eggs
> 2 medium onions
> 2 cloves garlic
> ½ tsp. nutmeg
> ¼ tsp. cloves
> 2 tbsps. brandy
> ¼ cup bread crumbs
> 3 bay leaves

Preheat oven to 350 degrees. Beat eggs, chop onions, mince garlic. Mix meat with all ingredients except bay leaves. Place in rectangular or circular baking dish (casserole will do) about 3–4" high. Place bay leaves on top of mixture. Cover with aluminum foil. Place in oven for 25 minutes. Remove aluminum foil; bake 10 minutes more until brown.

You may use mixture of ground beef with pork or veal.

VEAL

Veal Marsala
(with artichoke hearts, asparagus, or green or red pepper, or mushrooms)

(Preparation time: 10 minutes; 25 minutes cooking time)

Serves 4

This dish is an example of "module cooking" at its most flexible. It can be offered with three different vegetable components, one or all, and is as good with chicken breasts as with veal. It can be prepared an hour in advance, held, and assembled and cooked for serving in the last five minutes.

The key to success here is to use fine veal and force yourself to cook it a bit less than one would expect. Also you should take care that the mushrooms and other vegetables are not cooked beyond the point of near-crispness.

8 scallops of veal approximately 3" square and ¼" thick
2 tbsps. butter
2 tbsps. olive oil
½ cup marsala (or white wine or dry sherry)
½ cup beef broth
1 tsp. flour
salt and pepper
¼ lb. sliced mushrooms, fresh if possible and/or thinly sliced red or green pepper and/or 12 stalks of asparagus or 16 small mushrooms or package of frozen artichoke hearts

Dust 8 veal scallops in flour and sauté them in the butter and olive oil until they just lose their pinkness. Remove veal from pan and add wine, consommé or stock, salt and pepper. Scrape fragments of veal from the pan. Simmer 5 to 10 minutes, until sauce is consistency of heavy cream. If sauce fails to thicken, you may add another teaspoon of flour mixed to a paste with 2 tablespoons of water. At this point add veal and mushrooms, and vegetables. Simmer 7 minutes. While this dish is well worth making with canned mushrooms or asparagus, the peppers and artichoke hearts, the advantage of using fresh is not negligible.

Another variation:

Add 1½ tbsps. of lemon juice and lemon slices instead of vegetables.

Veal Parmigiana

(Preparation time: 30 minutes preparation and cooking time; add 20 minutes if you make a fresh tomato sauce contemporaneously)

Serves 4

8 small or 4 large veal cutlets
1 egg
1 cup bread crumbs
6 tbsps. Parmesan cheese, grated
3 tbsps. olive oil
1½ cups tomato sauce (see p. 131)
6 thin slices Mozzarella or Provolone cheese
salt and pepper

Either you or your butcher should pound the veal unless you are satisfied it is already very tender. (Rely on the butcher's word only if you and he have a prior meaningful relationship.)

Beat egg with fork, season with salt and pepper, place on one plate and put bread crumbs on another. Dip veal into egg and then into bread crumbs and then place gently into large frying pan in which oil has been heating. Brown each piece of veal on both sides over medium heat for 2–3 minutes, being sure that only one layer of veal is in pan at a time. (It may be necessary to stagger the use of oil if size of pan and number of veal slices requires a second browning session.) Avoid the temptation to *cook* the veal at this point; that comes later.

Place browned veal (with pan scrapings on top of each slice) in a single layer in one or more low-sided casseroles (a large pie-plate may be used) and cover each piece with about 2 tbsps. of tomato sauce. Place slice of cheese over each piece of veal so it pretty much covers it and sprinkle a tsp. of grated Parmesan over each slice. Bake at 350 degrees for 15 minutes or until cheese bubbles and begins to brown. Turn oven up to "broil" for no more than 3 minutes to brown and make some crust.

Grilled Veal Chops
(Preparation time: 3–4 minutes preparation;
20 minutes cooking time)

Serves 4

4 veal chops (loin) 1½" thick
2 tbsps. cooking oil
2 tbsps. dried rosemary

Heat broiler to hottest (10 minutes or more preheating will be necessary). Rub chops with oil and sprinkle rosemary equally on both sides. Broil first side 10 minutes, second side 8–9 minutes. Test one chop by making a small incision in the side. (All broilers do not heat equally.) If there is blood (or pink flesh) broil a bit longer until chops are bloodless.

Commentary:

Thick veal chops are so good and sufficiently unusual that we have set forth this recipe in violation of our general rule of excluding simple broiled preparations.

CHICKEN

Chicken With Tomatoes and White Wine
(Preparation time: 10 minutes, 30 minutes cooking time)

Serves 4–6

> 1 frying chicken cut into pieces
> flour
> salt and pepper
> dried thyme
> 2 tbsps. butter
> 2 tbsps. oil
> 1 bunch scallions, sliced
> ¼ lb. mushrooms chopped (or use canned chopped
>   mushrooms)
> ½ cup white wine
> ¾ cup canned tomatoes, chopped
> 2 tbsps. chopped parsley
> ¼ tsp. dry tarragon (if fresh not available)

Put flour, salt and pepper, and thyme in a paper bag. Shake chicken pieces in bag to coat with the flour. In a large skillet heat the butter and oil and brown the chicken on both sides.

Add everything else, cover and cook over a low flame for one half hour. Serve with rice or noodles.

Roast Chicken with Lemon and Subcutaneous Tarragon
(Preparation time: 10 minutes, 45 minutes cooking time)

Serves 4–6

1 roasting chicken (2–3 lbs.)
2 lemons
fresh tarragon
salt
black pepper

Rub salt and pepper inside chicken. Cut lemons in quarters and stuff into the chicken cavity. Tie up chicken legs to keep lemons from falling out. If you have fresh tarragon, loosen the chicken skin a little and tuck herb under as comprehensively as you can.

Roast for about an hour (depending on size) in 350 degree oven. Keep basting. Test for doneness by puncturing with a fork where leg meets thigh. When liquid runs clear it is done.

Chicken Tandoori Style
(Preparation time: 10–15 minutes marinating; 6–8 broiling time)

Serves 4–6

2 lbs. boneless chicken breasts

Follow recipe for steak tandoori (p. 83).
Broil 3–4 minutes on each side depending on thickness of chicken breasts.

Chicken Parmigiana

(Preparation time: 30 minutes preparation and cooking time; add 20 minutes if you make a fresh tomato sauce contemporaneously)

Follow the directions for veal parmigiana (p. 88) exactly, except the initial browning should be for 4 to 5 minutes instead of 2 to 3.

Chicken Mole

2 lbs. boneless chicken breasts
1 medium onion, quartered
1 carrot, chopped
4 cloves garlic, 2 sliced and 2 minced
1 bay leaf
3 tbsps. vegetable oil
2 corn tortillas
¼ cup sesame seeds
¼ cup raisins
3 tbsps. chili powder
¾ tsp. cinnamon
¾ tsp. ground cloves
½ tsp. cayenne pepper
2 squares semi-sweet chocolate
3 cups water
salt

In a saucepan place chicken breasts, carrot, onion, sliced garlic, 2 tsps. salt and water. Simmer 15 minutes. Remove chicken breasts, reserve broth. Remove and discard onion, carrot and garlic from broth. In a food processor liquify 2¾ cups of the broth, chili powder, the tortillas, the sesame seeds, raisins, cinnamon, cloves, cayenne, and minced garlic. Return to saucepan. Add the chocolate. Simmer for 10–12 minutes. When the liquid becomes viscous remove from heat. Slice chicken into thin shreds. Place in liquid and heat through. Serve.

Authors with Piglet

Authors without Piglet

Commentary:

Numerous variations are possible. Ground almonds maybe added to sauce and are good. Canned chicken broth somewhat reduces chicken poaching time (you don't have to deal with onion, carrot, garlic in broth). Bitter chocolate may be used instead of semi-sweet.

The regular recipe uses chilies anchos, which are really delicious but relatively hard to find. They take a long time to prepare—soaking, seeding, liquefying; the chili powder does very well.

Chicken Stuffed with Chicken
(Preparation time: 10–15 minutes preparation;
15–20 minutes cooking time)

4 boneless chicken breasts
¼ lb. mozzarella cheese
1 small onion
2 cloves garlic finely chopped
¼ cup chopped parsley
½ tsp. cayenne pepper
1 tsp. curry powder
2 limes

Preheat broiler. From each chicken breast trim away 2 ozs. of meat. Squeeze limes into a shallow dish, add curry powder to lime juice. Marinate larger pieces of chicken in lime juice, turning once or twice. Place the trimmed away meat, cheese, onion, garlic, parsley and cayenne pepper in food processor. Chop the mixture to a pasty consistency. In each of the marinating chicken breasts cut a small pocket, either in the side or into the top, cutting into and beneath the surface in all directions. Stuff the paste from the food processor into this pocket. Broil stuffed breasts on each side for 6–7 minutes until browned and stuffing is cooked through.

Commentary:

This is our adaptation, and a pretty good one, of chicken stuffed with chicken served at the Frontier Restaurant in New Delhi. Mozzarella approximates the Indian cheese.

Chinese Chicken

See Chinese beef and vegetables (p. 85).

Use chicken breasts instead of steak.

Chicken Breasts with Orange, Sherry and Soy
(Preparation time: 30–40 minutes)

Serves 4–6

4 whole boneless chicken breasts (each split in half)
½ cup orange juice
½ cup soy sauce
½ cup dry or medium sherry
2 cloves garlic
½ lb. fresh mushrooms
½ tsp. powdered ginger
5 tbsps. flour
4 tbsps. butter or margarine
salt and pepper

Mix orange juice, soy sauce, sherry, garlic and ginger in a large bowl. If convenient, marinate the chicken breasts in this mixture overnight or for several hours during the day. (You can put them in to soak while waiting for your coffee to heat before going to work in the morning. However, if you cannot arrange a lengthy marination, it is not at all serious).

Dust the breasts in flour which you have salted and peppered and place in a large saucepan with the melted butter or margarine. Brown at medium heat for five minutes and remove from pan to a warm plate. Pour in the liquid mixture (marinade if you have so used it) and cook it over a high heat while actively scraping with a wooden spoon the particles from browning the chicken breasts. In 3 to 5 minutes you will have a moderately thick sauce and should replace the chicken breasts and cook at a low bubble for about 20 minutes or a little longer, if they are not tender. Five minutes before completing the cooking of the chicken add the mushrooms which should be cut no smaller than halves or thirds depending on size. When ready to serve, this dish may sit on the stove while you are serving prior courses. If it does you should take into account that some additional cooking takes place as it sits or when you will heat it to serve, and should cook a bit less at first.

To serve, transfer from the pan to a large pre-warmed serving platter with the chicken and mushroom rich brown sauce displayed handsomely.

Will serve 4 generously, as it will provide each person with 2 half breasts. Judge your group and if one breast would be clearly enough, cut ingredients appropriately or freeze leftovers.

Pollo al Cognac
(Preparation time: one hour)

Serves 4

> 1 cut up large chicken
> 1 bottle of white wine *(cheap)*
> 6 garlic cloves *(whole,* not cup up)
> 2 leveled tsps. of ground black pepper
> 1 large onion (scored with cross incisions)
> 1 cup of water
> 2 tbsps. oil

Wash and salt well each piece of chicken. Brown on both sides in the oil in the same pot in which dish will be prepared. When browned, add to pot the garlic, onion, bottle of wine and water.

Then add the pepper, stir altogether, cover pot and cook on medium heat for 45 minutes.

When ready to serve, chicken should be accompanied by rice or french fried potatoes. Juice from pot should be served in espresso-sized coffee mugs along with the dish, to be drunk with meal.

Commentary:

The mystery is why it is called Pollo al Cognac. But our Chilean friend who introduced us to the dish says that's what it is.

Chicken Curry with Curry Sauce
(Preparation time: 20 minutes)

Serves 4–6

4 boneless chicken breasts
2 ozs. flour
1 tbsp. curry powder (more or less, depending on hotness)
4 tbsps. oil

Dry chicken breasts with paper towel. Slice into thin strips about ½″ wide, 2–3″ long. Mix 1 tbsp. curry powder (more or less depending on taste) with the flour. Thoroughly coat chicken with flour-curry powder mixture. Shake off excess flour. Heat oil. Thoroughly brown chicken in oil. Sauté about five minutes over medium flame, stirring so that flour-curry mixture does not burn. Chicken should be cooked through but not dried out. If you are serving with curry sauce, remove chicken from pan and set aside, keeping warm and covered in oven until sauce is cooked.

Curry Sauce
(Preparation time: 20–30 minutes)

1 small onion
1 large or two small garlic cloves
2 tbsps. oil
1 apple
1 banana
1 doz. almonds (preferably but not necessarily blanched)
1 tbsp. curry powder (more or less depending on hotness)
1 tbsp. chicken bouillon powder
2 cups water

Chop onion and garlic. Sauté in a saucepan in oil until limp. Peel and core apple. Chop apple and banana fine. If you are using a food processor turn into slush with the big blade. With a blender you may achieve the same result by chopping fine and placing in a blender with some of the water. Add apple and banana slush to onion and garlic along with chicken bouillon powder and curry powder and balance of the water. Chop almonds fine in food processor or crush with rolling pin or mortar and pestle, or chop fine and add to saucepan. Simmer 15 minutes or more. If sauce becomes too thick, add water.

Commentary:

True curry is custom made with ingredients varying according to each dish. It includes, or may include, turmeric, ginger, mace, cumin, cayenne pepper, fenugreek, cardamon, cinnamon, allspice, clove, etc. For quick and easy cooking pre-fabricated curry powder will have to do. Indians use it. When you have more time, consult an Indian cookbook for advanced version.

Chicken with Red and Green Peppers
(Preparation time: 15–20 minutes)

Serves 4–6

2 lbs. skinless, boned chicken breasts
1 red and 1 green pepper, sliced
3 scallions, chopped
3–4 tbsps. peanut or vegetable oil
1 tsp. ginger, chopped or ½ tsp. ginger powder
1 egg
soy sauce
sugar
sherry

Put sliced chicken into bowl; add chopped scallions and chopped ginger. Add egg and mix well. Then add sherry and marinate.

Meanwhile, heat oil. Add chicken mixture. Fry for 3–4 minutes. Add peppers. Stir. Mix well. Add soy sauce and sugar. Cook until done.

Chicken and Walnuts
(Preparation time: 20 minutes)

Serves 6

2 lbs. chicken breasts
1 egg
3 scallions
1 tsp. ginger or ½ tsp. powdered ginger
1 cup walnuts
hoisin sauce
hot sauce (optional)
4 tbsps. peanut or vegetable oil

Slice the cleaned, boned chicken breasts into ½″ strips. Put in bowl and combine with 1 beaten egg. Heat oil. Add walnuts. Stir for 2 minutes. Remove. Add ginger and scallions. Stir for 1 minute. Add chicken. Stir until done. Add walnuts and hoisin sauce. Add hot sauce if desired and serve.

Tatstaage (Japanese Fried Chicken)
(Preparation time: 15 minutes)

2 lbs. chicken breasts
1 cup cornstarch
2 tbsps. powdered ginger
6 tbsps. oil
1 tsp. salt
pepper to taste

Cut chicken breasts into about 1″ cubes. Dry in paper towel. Place cornstarch, ginger, salt and pepper in a paper bag. Put chicken cubes in bag. Shake. Heat oil in frying pan. Place cornstarch-ginger dusted chicken in pan. Don't crowd—you may do the job in batches. Turn until brown on all sides. Serve.

Commentary:

This is a terrific Japanese dish. The recipe was given to us by Pat, the owner of Fuji, in New York City. This may be where the idea for chicken McNuggets came from, but they are not as good. Tatstaage also may be made with small pieces of chicken hacked up, bones in, which has to fry a bit longer.

LAMB

Shish Kebab
(Preparation time: 10 minutes plus marinating time;
15 minutes cooking time)

Serves 6

3 lbs. of lamb from leg (ask butcher to remove fat and cut it in chunks for shish kebab)

For marinade:

1 tsp. salt
1 large clove garlic, mashed
½ cup chopped onion
1 tsp. oregano
¼ tsp. black pepper
¼ cup salad or olive oil
⅓ cup sherry, vinegar or lemon juice

Place lamb pieces in marinade, turning frequently. You can marinate one hour or as long as overnight. (If you have a lot of lamb, you may have to double the marinade recipe). Put lamb pieces on skewers. Broil 12–15 minutes turning to brown all sides. At the same time, broil pieces of green or red peppers, tomato chunks or cherry tomatoes, small parboiled white onions or the boiled onions that can be purchased in jars.

Commentary:

This is a summer favorite, best when charcoal grilled. If you're rained out, it's ok to broil kebabs in broiler. Since the vegetables have a habit of falling off skewers, we have given up trying to alternate them with the meat and grill or broil them separately.

We serve this with rice, substituting the marinade liquid for some of the water needed for cooking rice. Add some drained canned mushrooms or sautéed fresh sliced mushrooms to rice.

Lamb Curry
(Preparation time: 15 minutes)

2 lbs. lamb in 2″ cubes
1 cup flour
1 tbsp. curry powder
2 cloves garlic
4 tbsps. oil
curry sauce (see p. 97)

Place flour, curry powder and lamb in paper bag. Shake to coat lamb with flour-curry powder mixture. Mince garlic, heat oil in pan, brown garlic in oil. Brown lamb cubes in hot oil. Sauté for 7–8 minutes. Serve with curry sauce.

Tandoori Lamb
(Preparation time: marinate 20 minutes, broil 5–6 minutes)

2 lbs. lamb in 2″ cubes

Follow recipe for tandoori steak (see p. 83). Test for doneness (we prefer it a bit pink) after cubes have broiled 5–6 minutes.

Noisette of Lamb
(Preparation time: 5 minutes; 15 minutes cooking time)

Serves 4

Probably one of the most elegant and easiest main courses, a noisette of lamb is like a beef tenderloin, completely boneless and—unlike a rack of lamb—simple to carve. Order one noisette for four people.

Heat oven to 450 degrees. Sprinkle rosemary (fresh or dry) on lamb and rub it in. Put noisette(s) in oven, turn oven down to 350 degrees and watch carefully. We use a meat thermometer and start checking at 120 degrees (very rare). If you like lamb rosy rare (and we hope you don't like it better done than that), let it go to 125 degrees.

Commentary:

Noisettes are great with a pureed vegetable (p. 151) and a half tomato with a slice of chevre cheese on top (broiled for a few minutes until cheese browns).

Lamb in Almond Cream Sauce
(Preparation time: 30 minutes preparation;
12–15 minutes cooking time)

Serves 4–6

2 lbs. lamb (preferably from leg)
8 ozs. yogurt
1 tbsp. fennel or anise seeds
2 medium to large onions
2 large cloves garlic
2 tbsps. chopped fresh ginger or 1 tbsp. dried ginger
1 doz. almonds
4 tbsps. oil
8 ozs. sweet cream
handful chinese parsley (also called cilantro or fresh
          coriander, or use flat ordinary parsley)

Cut lamb into small cubes, about ½″ in each dimension. The smaller the pieces the quicker the marination and cooking time. Chop half of the onions, garlic, ginger (if fresh), parsley. Mix with yogurt and lamb cubes. Marinate at room temperature 20 minutes or more. Sauté the remaining half of the onions and garlic in the oil for 5 or 6 minutes. Add the lamb and marinade. Stir while browning on all sides. Cover. Cook covered over low flame 5 or 6 minutes more. Crush or chop almonds fine. Add almonds and cream. Simmer until thick. Serve.

Meatballs in Egg-Lemon Sauce/Youvarlakia
(a la Olga Gellhorn)
(Preparation time: 1 hour)

Serves 4

    1½ lb. ground lamb (or veal or beef)
    1 onion, grated
    2 tbsps. minced parsley
    ½ cup uncooked rice
    1 tbsp. crushed mint
    1 egg, beaten
    1 can beef consommé or broth
    butter
    salt and pepper
    egg-lemon sauce

Combine ground meat, onion, mint, rice and egg; season with salt and pepper; knead well; then form into small balls, about walnut size. Roll balls in minced parsley. In a deep pot melt 4 tbsps. butter and arrange meatballs in rows in the bottom of the pot; add broth, 2 cups water and another 2 tbsps. butter. Season with salt and pepper, and simmer covered for 35 to 40 minutes. Remove from fire and add egg-lemon sauce according to instructions in egg-lemon recipe, below. Return to stove and keep over a low fire until ready to serve. (Greeks serve as soup with a crusty bread, feta slices, Greek olives, white wine).

Egg-Lemon Sauce (Avgolemono)
(2 cups)
(Preparation time: 15–20 minutes)

    3 eggs, separated
    juice of 2 lemons
    1 cup broth or stock
    1 tbsp. cornstarch

Basic Greek sauce, over vegetables, fish, meats. Use stock of vegetables or meat or canned broth or diluted chicken stock base. Beat egg whites until stiff, add egg yolks and continue beating. Add lemon juice very slowly, beating so as not to curdle. Thicken hot chicken broth with cornstarch dissolved in a little water; slowly add boiling stock to egg mixture, beating constantly until smooth and creamy and serve over cooked fish, vegetables, meat.

PORK

Pork and Oysters
(Preparation time: 20–25 minutes)

Serves 6

2 lbs. lean boneless pork loin
20 oysters (shucked)
1 tbsp. ginger minced fine or 1 tsp. ginger powder
3–4 scallions, chopped
4 tbsps. peanut or vegetable oil
2 tbsps. soy sauce
sugar
3 ozs. sherry
3 ozs. water

Heat oil. Add chopped scallion and sauté for 1 minute. Cut pork into 2″ cubes, add to oil. Stir pork until it browns. Then add oysters. Add soy sauce, ginger, sherry and sugar. Cover. Simmer for 15 minutes. Stir from time to time. If too dry add a little water. Check for seasoning and serve.

Pork Chops with Sweet and Hot Peppers
(Preparation time: 25 minutes; 20–30 minutes cooking time)

Serves 4

2 lbs. pork chops ½" thick
1 large sweet green pepper
2 tbsp. sliced hot green pepper, e.g., chilies serranos or
      jalapeños (more or less according to taste)
½ tsp. ground cloves
½ tsp. ground cinnamon
Chinese parsley (also called fresh coriander or cilantro)—
      fresh parsley may be used if Chinese parsley is not
      available
8 ozs. yogurt
4 tbsps. oil
salt

Cut sweet peppers into thin strips. Slice hot peppers into very thin strips, adjusting quantity to taste. Mix with yogurt, cloves, cinnamon. Coat pork chops with mixture and marinate at room temperature 20 minutes. Heat oil in large skillet. Brown chops on both sides. Your chops will probably occupy two layers in the pan so you may have to remove half of them as you brown the remainder. Place all browned chops back in the pan. Add marinade. Reduce heat. Cover. Cook over medium-low flame until green peppers are soft—about 15 minutes or more.

Sprinkle with chopped Chinese or regular parsley. Salt to taste.

Grilled Pork Medallions
(Preparation time: 10 minutes; 10 minutes cooking time)

Serves 4

1 boneless loin of pork, about 1½ lbs.
¼ cup olive oil
2 tbsps. red wine vinegar
salt and pepper to taste
1 tsp. dried or fresh rosemary
1 tsp. dried cumin
melted butter, if desired

Slice the pork into eight pieces approximately the same thickness. Combine all other ingredients except the butter to form a marinade. Add pork slices. Heat the grill and cook pork turning often for about 10 minutes. Brush with butter as you grill.

CHAPTER VII

Fish

PRESENTATION, BONING, GARNISHES

The presentation is most impressive when the whole fish is served on a large platter or board (constructed to trap run-off juices and sauce), with sauce and/or garnish spooned over it, reserving some, if there is not enough room, for a sauce boat. Carrot rounds, parsley, perhaps dill, add color and flavor.

Boning the fish can be learned only with experience, because different species have distinct bone structures. If you have a relationship of trust and confidence with your fishmonger, ask him/her to show you how to bone the particular fish you've bought. If you don't have such a relationship or if you don't speak the same language (sometimes the case) try the following:

After cooking, with the back of the fish near you and the belly away from you probe gently into the backbone area (slightly above the bone) with a large spoon (the edges of the spoon should be parallel not perpendicular to the table), making an incision along the length of the back, pushing the spoon into the flesh until it touches the backbone. Then place the spoon in contact with the backbone and move it towards the belly along the ribs. This will separate the flesh from the bone on most fish. Then lift off. Repeat until all flesh is removed. Flat fish have a fringe of small sharp bones around their circumference which should be pared away with the spoon and discarded. It's easy after the second or third time. If, however, the exercise continues to flummox you, ask the fishmonger to bone the fish when you buy it, leaving head on.

Baked Whole Bluefish

(Preparation time: 20 minutes; 10 minutes cooking time per inch of thickness)

    4–6 lb. bluefish, striped bass or other whole fish this size,
        boned, head on
onions, sliced thin
2 green peppers, sliced thin
2 tomatoes, sliced

Stuff the fish with the vegetables, add sprigs of parsley and other fresh herbs, if available. Close the fish by skewering with toothpicks or tie it up. You can bake the fish in the oven at 400 degrees or grill it outside. Timing: about 10 minutes per inch of thickness plus extra time for the stuffing. You simply will have to test for doneness.

Serve with lemon slices or lemon butter.

Baked Bluefish Provencale

(Preparation time: 15–20 minutes;
10 minutes cooking time per inch of thickness)

Serves 4–6

    4–5 lb. bluefish, cleaned, scaled, head(s) on
2 cups chopped onion
2 tomatoes
4 cloves garlic
12 pitted olives
6 tbsps. olive oil
2 bay leaves
1 tbsp. oregano
½ cup white wine

Preheat oven to 400 degrees. Chop onions, cut tomatoes in eighths, mince garlic. Sauté onions and tomatoes in 4 tbsps. of the oil. Place bluefish in baking dish. Pour wine in dish. Add bay leaves and oregano. Rub top of fish with 2 tbsps. of oil and spread minced garlic over it. Place in oven. If fish is at or near room temperature bake 10 minutes for each inch of thickness at the thickest point, i.e. if fish is 2" thick, bake 20 minutes. If below room temperature, bake somewhat longer. When you think it is done, insert sharp knife at backbone. If flesh is white and no blood appears it is done.

Heat onion, tomato and olives for 2 minutes. Pour over fish. Serve from baking pan.

Fish Tandoori Style
(Preparation time: 30 minutes;
12 minutes cooking time per inch of thickness)

Serves 4–6

1 three to four lb. striped bass, bluefish, flounder or other fish
4 ozs. lemon or lime juice
1 tsp. cayenne pepper
2 large cloves garlic
1 onion, chopped
2 ozs. yogurt
1 medium or 2 small tomatoes (canned or fresh), chopped
salt

Prick fish with sharp point of knife. Crush garlic, mix with salt and pepper, rub into fish. Place in a dish with lemon or lime juice, turn several times.

After 20 minutes or more, dry with paper towel. Mix yogurt, onion and tomato together. Cover one side of fish with ½ of the yogurt-onion-tomato mixture.

Place in flame proof baking dish in a very hot pre-heated broiler, yogurt coated side up. The total broiling time should be 12 minutes per inch of thickness of the fish at the thickest point of the fish. When half of the total broiling time has passed, turn the fish over. Use a broad spatula or two to effect the turnover, being careful to avoid breaking the fish. Coat the second side with the remainder of the yogurt mixture.

Standard timing for broiling fish is 10 minutes per inch of thickness. The extra 2 minutes is to allow for the yogurt insulation. If the fish is very cold another minute or two may be needed. You can tell if fish is done by inserting a knife in its back to the bone and observing whether the juices are clear and the flesh white. If so, it is done. If the juices are pink and the flesh translucent, allow to cook until they become clear and the flesh is white.

Shrimp Creole
(Preparation time: 10 minutes; 35 minutes cooking time)

Serves 4–6

2½ lb. shrimp
2 large onions, chopped
1 green pepper, chopped
1 large clove garlic
2 tbsps. olive oil
2 tbsps. peanut oil
1 can tomato paste
1 large can of tomatoes
¼ cup parsley chopped
crushed chili peppers (according to taste)
1 tsp. oregano

Heat oils and sauté onions, pepper, and garlic until onion is golden. Add tomato paste, tomatoes and herbs and spices. Simmer until thick, about a half hour. Meanwhile, peel shrimp and add towards end, for about 3–4 minutes of cooking. Do not overcook shrimp. Add a little more oregano and serve over rice.

Shrimp or Scallop Curry
(Preparation time: 5 minutes; 5 minutes cooking time)

Serves 4–6

> 2 lbs. shrimp, sea or bay scallops (if sea scallops cut into
>   smaller pieces)
> 1 cup flour
> 2 tbsps. curry powder (more or less, depending on hotness)
> 4 tbsps. oil

Dust scallops or peeled shrimp in flour-curry powder mixture—best done by shaking together in a paper bag. Sauté shrimp 4–5 minutes in hot oil; scallops 2–3 minutes. Serve

Curry Sauce

See Curry Sauce recipe above, p. 97. But, instead of chicken bouillon use either 2 cups clam juice or 1 cup sweet cream or 1 cup clam juice and ½ cup sweet cream, simmered until mixture thickens.

Oriental Fried Shrimp
(Preparation time: 20 minutes, mostly spent peeling shrimp; less time if you buy them peeled; 10 minutes cooking time)

Serves 4–6

> 2 lbs. medium shrimp
> 6 tbsps. soy sauce
> 2 ozs. cornstarch
> 2 cloves garlic,

and/or

1 oz. fresh ginger grated or
1 tsp. ginger powder

(See below for discussion of these options)

8 oz. cooking oil

Peel shrimp (devein only if you feel it aesthetically preferable—we don't), leaving tails on. Cut 2 or 3 slits on each side. Pat dry with paper towel. Mix soy sauce with either pressed garlic *or* grated ginger, *or* if you like, both. Bring soy sauce to a simmer. Marinate shrimp in soy-garlic and/or ginger mixture at least 5 minutes, but as long as convenient. You might perform this phase the night or morning before

Drain, reserve soy sauce liquid. Pat dry with paper towel. Dust with cornstarch. If you are using ginger powder rather than grated fresh ginger, mix it with the cornstarch before dusting. This is done conveniently by placing cornstarch in large paper bag, adding shrimp and shaking thoroughly.

Heat oil in saucepan which is small enough so that the oil is at least 1½–2″ deep. If you have a deep fryer, use it. Heat oil until it is so hot that water sprinkled on it skips along surface. Put shrimp in oil, 4–6 at a time (putting too many in at once cools the oil excessively) and fry about a minute until golden brown. Remove with slotted spoon and place on paper towel to blot up excess oil.

Serve with reserved soy sauce as a dip.

Shrimp and Snowpeas
(Preparation time: 30 minutes)

Serves 6

> 2½ dozen medium sized shrimp
> 3 scallions
> ½ lb. snowpeas
> peanut oil or vegetable oil
> 1 egg
> sherry
> scallions
> salt

Clean shrimp. Put the cleaned shrimp into a bowl. Add sherry and beaten egg. Mix. Marinate in refrigerator for 30 minutes.

Meanwhile heat oil. Add chopped scallions and sauté for 1 minute. Then add shrimp mixture and continue to stir for about 4 minutes. Add snowpeas and season with salt and continue to cook for about 5 minutes.

Poached Fish with Garnish
(Preparation time: 20 minutes preparation;
15–25 minutes cooking time)

Serves 4–6

> 1 cleaned and scaled bluefish, seabass, flounder, striped bass,
>   sea trout, 4–5 lbs. or 2 smaller fish (e.g. red snapper)
>   adding up to same weight, with head not removed
> 16 ozs. clam juice
> 1 cup white wine
> 1 onion
> 1 carrot
> 2 cloves garlic
> 2 bay leaves
> 1 tbsp. oregano

Place clam juice and wine in a fish poacher or pan large enough to accommodate fish. Peel and quarter onion, cut carrot into 1″ pieces, peel and chop garlic coarsely, add to pan along with bay leaves and oregano and bring to boil, reduce to simmer for 10 minutes. Add fish to pot, simmer for a time equivalent to 10 minutes per inch of thickness at the thickest part. If the fish was very cold at time of immersion it will take a bit longer. Test by inserting the point of a sharp blade in backbone. If flesh is white, and there is no blood, fish is done. Otherwise poach a bit longer.

Remove and serve with garnish: see below.

Grilled Swordfish
(Preparation time: 1–2 hours marinating;
10 minutes cooking time per inch of thickness)

Serves 4

    Swordfish steaks (1½ lbs. for four persons)
    2 tbsps. olive oil
    3 tbsps. lemon juice
    3 garlic cloves, mashed

Combine oil, lemon juice and garlic for a marinade. Marinate the swordfish between one and two hours. (In an emergency less time will do). Grill over charcoal and, before serving, grind lots of black pepper over the fish.

Commentary:

This recipe comes from Stella Heffron, a Washington, D.C. cook and one of the best we know. Her approach to food: Keep it simple.

Salmon Teriyaki

(Preparation time: 8 minutes or longer, if you make your own Teriyaki sauce)

Serves 6

> 6 salmon steaks (about 1" thick)
> 1 tbsp. Teriyaki sauce
> 1 tbsp. sunflower oil

First brown the salmon steaks in hot oil for about 2 minutes each side in a good quality non-stick frying pan. Remove the steaks and pour the Teriyaki sauce into the pan. Boil for about 2 minutes. Return the steaks to the pan and cook for about 3 minutes, turning them frequently and taking care not to overcook. Ideally the center should be almost raw.

Commentary:

The work of another Dean, Jeffrey Jowell, formerly Dean of the Faculty of Law at London University, who adds: "You can usually buy your Teriyaki sauce ready-made. However, in England any item is likely to be out of stock for no obvious rhyme or reason. So why not concoct your own Teriyaki sauce out of soya sauce, rice wine, honey and condiments of your own choosing."

SAUCES AND GARNISHES

Poached or steamed fish usually are completed by serving them with a sauce or garnish. Varieties are virtually infinite and methods vary considerably. Herewith follow a few basic sauces, with suggestions about how they may be varied.

The sauce may be served separately, or if you are sure everyone will like it, poured over the fish before serving.

Aioli
(Preparation time: 10 minutes)

A garlic mayonnaise. The recipe appears on p. 48.

Ravigotte
(Preparation time: 5–10 minutes)

A vinaigrette with additional ingredients such as capers, anchovies, pickles, herbs. The recipe appears on p. 47.

Shallot Butter
(Preparation time: 5 minutes)

    6 ozs. sweet butter
    1 shallot chopped very fine
    1 tbsp. lemon or white wine

Warm butter until soft, mix in shallots, lemon juice or wine. Chopped parsley may be added. A cup of bottled clam juice or the liquid from the fish poaching, reduced by ¾ by vigorous boiling, then cooled, may be added.

Garlic Butter
(Preparation time: 5 minutes)

    6 ozs. sweet butter
    1 shallot chopped very fine
    1 large or small cloves garlic, chopped very fine

Warm butter until soft, mix in shallot and garlic. Chopped parsley may be added. A cup of bottled clam juice, reduced by ¾ by vigorous boiling, then cooled, may be added.

Seafood Garnish
(Preparation time: 15–20 minutes)

3–4 clams, mussels or shrimp per person or combination
 thereof
1 shallot, small onion or scallion, chopped
1 clove garlic
½ tsp. thyme
1 bay leaf
½ cup white wine

Scrub mussels and/or clams and if using mussels cut away
beards. Place all ingredients in saucepan. Cover. Turn heat high.
After shellfish open, allow to cool, remove from liquid, cut clams
or mussels away from shell, rinse in broth the shellfish have given
off to remove residual sand, if any.

The same procedure may be followed with shrimp. Place them
in the wine-shallot-herb-liquid and simmer until they turn pink—a
few minutes. Remove from liquid. When cool, peel off shells.

Strain liquid and return it to pan. Reduce by half over high,
high heat until slightly thickened.

Now, return the shellfish or shrimp to the liquid and pour
over the poached fish, or serve separately, from a sauce boat. Or
add to garlic or shallot butter, mix together and pour over fish.

Mushroom Sauce
(Preparation time: 15 minutes)

1 lb. mushrooms sliced
1 clove garlic chopped
4 ozs. butter
2 ozs. olive or other oil

Melt butter in oil, sauté garlic until soft. Add mushrooms, sauté over high, high heat until mushrooms give off liquid, reduce liquid until mushrooms turn slightly brown. Place 8 ozs. of clam juice in a saucepan. Reduce by half. Add mushrooms. Pour over fish or serve separately.

Green Sauce
(Preparation time: 20 minutes)

With a food processor, green sauce takes a few minutes. Otherwise it takes a long time (with mortar and pestle) and is not recommended if you are under time constraints.

½ lb. spinach (frozen spinach may be used) or romaine lettuce
½ lb. watercress or swiss chard or endive
4 anchovy filets
2 tbsps. capers
2 tbsps. vinegar
*1 tbsp. dried tarragon or thyme
*1 handful chopped fresh herbs
*1 handful fresh parsley
4 ozs. olive oil
2 ozs. bottled clam juice
salt
pepper

*Other herbs in various combinations may be used.

Boil greens together five minutes. Squeeze dry. Place in food processor with large blade in place. Liquify, add other ingredients, dribbling oil in last, slowly, until the mixture becomes thick and somewhat mayonnaise-like. Use somewhat more than 4 ozs. oil if necessary to achieve the right consistency.

CHAPTER VIII

Theory and Practice of Pasta

PASTA

Kinds of pasta. Home made is best, but a lot of work and time consuming. It is so much better than any other kind, however, that it is worth the effort. Nevertheless, it cannot fall within the time constraints we have imposed on ourselves for this book. Food processors and pasta machines speed things up, but even with these aids, fresh pasta is a task for weekend leisure or, perhaps, time-cost effective if made in large batches and frozen.

Fresh pasta is now widely available, sometimes frozen, as it has been in Italy and France and some stores in Italian neighborhoods in the United States. Lately, frozen pasta, as good as the fresh, has been available in some specialty shops and supermarkets.

The conventional wisdom is that imported brands are better than the better domestic ones. But the differences are often so marginal as to escape our detection.

Cooking Time. Pasta is always best *al dente,* or quite firm. We find that usually it should be cooked less than the minimum time recommended on the box. Place one lb. of pasta in a very large quantity of boiling water, six quarts or more, if you have a pot that large. A tablespoon of oil in the water and frequent picking apart with a long fork prevent the strands from sticking together. Well before the minimum time recommended on the box, extract a strand or piece and taste it. If it is tender enough to eat, remove from water. If not, give it a little more time and test often.

Types of Pasta. The varieties are enormous: e.g., spaghetti, spagettini, linguini, fettucini, ziti, fusilli, etc., etc. Any standard pasta manual lists them all, (not really—it is not possible to list all). You can do almost as well by browsing on the shelves at an Italian grocer where considerable variety is on display. There are conventions, e.g., clam sauce should be eaten on linguini, bolognese sauces on spaghetti, sauce Alfredo on fettucini. But, actually, any sauce may be combined with any pasta with good results. A useful principle is that sauces with lumps (chicken liver, sausage, broccoli), go better with pastas of more complex shape, e.g., with spirals, holes, cogs or declivities, the little chunks in the sauce getting trapped in the interstices, etc. Thicker sauces, e.g., Alfredo, do well on broad noodles, e.g., fettucini, which they can coat copiously as distinguished from, let us say, thin spaghettini, which they might swamp. But these are suggestions, not injunctions. Common sense is a good guide. If you find yourself at home on a rainy night with only a box of spaghettini and ingredients for sauce Alfredo, you can do very well.

Multiple Pasta Presentation. A tantalizing first course or serious main event may be made of three different pastas (or two) with different sauces, several simultaneously or in sequence. Different shapes and thicknesses of pasta and (three or two) different sauces, e.g., vegetable, meat and fish make a splash. The work and time can be minimal, although you mess up a lot of pots and dishes (if you serve on separate plates, in sequence). An obvious tactic is to *start* by boiling the water—4 to 6 quarts take quite a while to bring to a boil. While it heats toward the boiling point you can make the sauces.

Impromptu Pasta Sauce Principles: a synthesis. Pasta sauces come in endless variety. A few general principles will allow anyone to compose his/her own out of ingredients that may be at hand. Some books go on and on, using virtually every ingredient imaginable. But the genus seems to shake down into a number of species: meat, seafood, vegetable, cream and other. Some subspecies exist, e.g., tomato, shrimp, beef. And there is a good deal of cross-breeding like tomato sauce with beef, vegetable with cream, and so forth. Oriental sauces are quite something else. Depending on how viscous or liquid you prefer your sauce it may have to be combined with something soupier to douse the pasta completely or with a thickener. This is discussed below in Viscosity/Liquidity.

NOTE: IMPORTANT: WARNING. Since we will be discussing a large number of ingredients, procedures and combinations, read this section in full before undertaking any ventures suggested in it.

VEGETABLES

Potatoes. Potatoes are virtually a substantive, not a saucing factor. They may be substituted for up to ½ the weight of the pasta you might prepare. Small red potatoes should first be boiled 15 minutes, sliced or quartered, maybe then sautéd in onions and garlic and used in place of some of the pasta.

Garlic and Onions. Chopping and sautéing in oil or butter is a good start for many sauces. *Leeks, shallots, scallions,* any of all of these, if they are on hand, may be used in place of or in addition to onion. Flavors vary somewhat, as do texture and appearance. Dried minced garlic and onion (first soaked in hot water) are acceptable substitutes.

Carrots. Slice thin (or chop) and sauté in oil or butter, usually with onions and garlic. Carrots contribute color and flavor, but even if sliced very thin they must sauté at least 10 minutes to become tender.

Red Peppers, Green Peppers (sweet). Either or both may be chopped and sautéed in oil or butter with any or all of the above. They add flavor and color. A small hot pepper, very finely minced adds surprise.

Tomatoes. The tomato question may be crucial, for it can determine the dominant characteristic of your sauce. If you use a lot of tomatoes you will have a tomato sauce of one sort or another. A small quantity merely gives the sauce a touch of tomato flavor. Two principles: unless the tomato season is at its height and you have access to terrific ones, canned are superior. Second, tomatoes profit by long simmering, causing the liquid to reduce considerably. There is the "whether to skin and/or seed or purée" issue. We take no position on this question. Some object to seed and skin on aesthetic grounds. Time should be the determining factor. (If you decide to skin and/or seed, 10–20 seconds in boiling water or on a fork over an open flame loosens the skin. If you are skinning only one tomato it will be quicker to rotate it on a long fork over a flame until skin bursts. Cool, peel, quarter. With your index finger dislodge and discard seeds).

Tomato purée works. Pomi, an imported tomato purée, which comes in a box, is very useful. We also have used tomato juice, simmering longer to thicken. Tomatoes should simmer with onion, garlic, bay leaf, herbs until thickened. Tomato paste has the virtue of being thick and herb flavored to start with and may be added to enhance a tomato sauce. Tomato paste in toothpaste-like tubes is easy to use.

Because you may be accustomed to pasta sauces with tomato is no reason to feel it is mandated. You have freedom of choice and may want a tomatoless sauce.

Celery. Good to add in a late phase of simmering, chopped so that it retains crunchiness.

Nuts. Celery crunchiness reminds us of nuts. Almonds, filberts, pecans, walnuts, etc. impart crunchiness and flavor and should be added late in the cooking process so as not to become soggy. If time is not pressing, you could toast or sauté first.

Olives. Green olives, pitted, chopped roughly are good to add in late phase of simmering so that they don't become soft. Olives stuffed with pimentos look good, don't taste different, really. Black semi dried olives are good, too.

Peas. Scatter them in the sauce near the end of cooking. It makes the sauce, particularly those light in color, look pretty and taste crisp. The peas add sweetness. Frozen peas defrost quickly in the sauce.

Capers. Distinctive flavor, rather salty. Should be rinsed. Good to add late so they preserve identity and don't decompose.

Other Vegetables. Broccoli or cauliflower flowerlets and thinly sliced stems of both, asparagus tips and their diagonally, thinly sliced stems (first discarding thick woody ends), artichoke hearts, canned, fresh or laboriously extracted from the artichoke, and other vegetables may go into the sauce. If you want to take the time, the vegetables may be sautéed first in oil and with garlic. Their flavor becomes more distinctive.

Eggplant presents a separate question. It takes well, we think, only to combining with garlic, onion, tomato and meats. Skin, then cube a medium eggplant, sauté at least 20 minutes in oil. Go heavy on the chopped garlic. Salt and pepper to taste. The smaller the cubes the less time you need to sauté. You may chop very fine in a food processor. But eggplant takes a fair amount of cooking, so 20 minutes is a minimum.

Mushrooms should be sautéed separately before putting in

sauce as the process concentrates their flavor. Oil and juices from sautéing should be scraped from pan into sauce too. The mushroom sautéing process has been prescribed variously. We prefer quartering, salting, stirring rapidly over very high heat until the mushrooms exude liquid, stirring further over lower heat until liquid is almost entirely reduced. You might, if garlic is not being used otherwise (or even if it is), sauté garlic in the oil for a minute or two before adding the mushrooms.

CAUTION: LESS IS MORE. TWO OR THREE OR ONLY A FEW MORE VEGETABLES ARE PREFERABLE TO EVERYTHING YOU CAN LAY YOUR HANDS ON.

Anchovies, discussed below with seafood, cross most boundaries and may be stirred into many sauces as a flavoring. An anchovy or anchovy and garlic sauce is very good. Anchovies in a tomato sauce go well, and they are often combined with tomato, olives, capers, etc. to make sauces in the style of Provence. See bagna cauda, supra p. 49.

MEAT

Prosciutto. Elegant, expensive, delicious. Chop, sauté, add to a basic vegetable sauce. It goes well with most seafood sauces. Smoked hams (e.g. Smithfield) are flavorful. Ordinary ham not bad, either.

Sausages. These include breakfast, sweet, hot, chorizo, kielbasi, pepperoni, bratwurst and any other. Prick holes in whole small sausages. Slice large ones. Prick holes with a fork, cook in water to cover until it evaporates. Allow fat to melt away. Brown lightly. Pour off fat. Cut into ½ to 1″ slices. Add to sautéed vegetable and/or onion and/or garlic base. May be combined with other meats.

Chicken. Boned chicken breasts best for quick results. Sauté small chunks or strips. When brown, add to a basic vegetable sauce. If you have a bit more time, chicken may be poached in water with onion, garlic, bay leaf, herbs, pepper, celery and/or other vegetables. Disjointed chicken poaches faster. Remove flesh from bone, shred. Add to tomato, garlic or other sauce.

Beef. Thin strips or small cubes of steak, browned, may be added to sauce. Ground beef sautéed, fat poured off, is very good added to a vegetable sauce. Ground beef is conventional in a tomato sauce but need not be confined to it. This makes sauce Bolognese.

Bacon. Can be used like sausages or in combination with other meats. Cut into 1 or 2″ squares. Fry, pour off fat. Add to sautéed vegetables and/or onions and/or garlic.

FISH AND SEAFOOD

Seafood flavors are more delicate than others we have discussed. Cooking times are shorter. A number of principles should be observed. *One:* seafood or fish should be extraordinarily fresh. Nevertheless, canned seafood—e.g., clams—does not offend in a pasta sauce, as it would in most other mediums and you can use canned clams, mussels, tuna fish, sardines, if in a hurry, you can't go out and you want to make something interesting. *Two:* scrub clams or mussels, soak as long as possible before cooking for (several hours, but you can get away with no soaking if you remove meat from shell and rinse throughly in the clam or mussel liquid after cooking). Place in pot with no water, a garlic clove or two, assorted herbs, pepper, a few ounces of wine. Cook over high heat until shells open. Allow to cool, remove clams or mussels from shells, strain liquid (removing sand, grit, etc.) and add to vegetable base. (Some chopped ham or prosciutto would not be out of order.) Shrimps should be shelled (no need to devein, although aesthetes do), simmered until they turn pink in wine-garlic-herb liquid. They may then be chopped and added to sauce.

Fish. Cut sole, bass or other filets into ½″ chunks, simmer in butter or oil with garlic until brown. You may add chopped prosciutto or ham. Canned tuna or sardines may be sautéed briefly.

LIQUIDITY/VISCOSITY

The vegetables, meat, fish or possible combinations thereof may be combined with the pasta as a soupy or somewhat dry sauce or in an intermediate fluid state. The sauce could be made thick or free flowing. For example, a butter or olive oil sauce, perhaps with garlic or anchovies may only coat the pasta strands. Or a clam or mussel or tomato sauce may provide soupy liquid to be spooned up or soaked up in bread. There are various possibilities. Here we discuss some of them.

Butter or Oil. A simple sauce is plain butter or oil. This may be combined with, to be basic, garlic, anchovy or both, or with one or more of the ingredients discussed above to become a complex vegetable, meat or seafood sauce. The flavored oil coats the pasta and causes the other ingredients to adhere to it. But the liquid content will be minimal.

Tomato Sauce. Tomato sauce alone, or combined with one or more of the ingredients discussed above is quite common. Meat, fish, vegetables or perhaps a combination of several is not unusual in tomato broth. You may use a lot or a little. If there is a lot, the soup may be spooned or sopped up with bread.

Stocks. Fish stock, chicken or beef stock (or clam juice or bouillon powder, as substitutes) are good for simmering some of the basic ingredients. (Fish stock with fish, chicken stock with chicken, etc.) Again, spooning or sopping may follow consumption of the pasta.

Wine. White or red wine may be combined with stocks, and/or added to other ingredients and simmered.

Cream. Heavy sweet cream may be added to most sauces, simmered until thickened. Sometimes, as with Sauce Alfredo, egg yolks may be added, but only after removing from heat, lest they harden.

Thickening. A bit of flour in water, or flour combined with butter may be mixed into a sauce to make it thicker. A tablespoon of cornstarch or arrowroot, predissolved in water or sauce liquid, does it better.

Simmering, uncovered, has a thickening effect too. Reduces liquid and concentrates flavor.

HERBS AND SPICES

Several principles are useful. Fresh herbs are much much better than dried. Fresh parsley usually is available and a bunch, chopped, is a positive addition to most sauces. Virtually all herbs are interchangeable. Certainly, different herbs' tastes vary (sometimes only somewhat) but a recipe or concept which calls for oregano will be good (although different) with tarragon or thyme. (A few, like mint or cilantro, are so distinctive that this rule doesn't apply.) Spices are not as interchangeable, but they do come in sort of families. Cinnamon, cloves, allspice, nutmeg may be substituted for one another. (Again, they are different, but acceptable results will follow if one is used for another.) We prefer whole cinnamon sticks, peppercorns, cloves, nutmeg and allspice (grated to order) to their preground versions. These add interest if used very lightly in meat or vegetable sauces or ground or grated and dusted lightly on cream sauces. Dried herbs and spices are better if toasted lightly in a pan before using.

Piquancy. Hot peppers, red, green, fresh or canned, tabasco, etc. may be added to taste, if you like. But reactions to hot sauce vary widely and you should know your audience well before you start down this road.

CHEESES

Grated cheese is excellent on most pastas (conventionally, seafood sauces are excluded from the treatment). It is by far preferable to grate to order. Parmesan is best and the best of it is outrageously expensive. Often we substitute romano, asiago (also expensive) or raclette. Swiss, or one of its variants (e.g., emmenthaler), serves well. Softer cheese, e.g., mozarella or swiss melt nicely on a pasta dish if placed in oven. This goes well over a tomato sauce.

NOTE ON ALL OF THE ABOVE:

A dozen forays into pasta making experiments, starting with only a few ingredients, escalating slowly, eschewing junk laden combinations, so that you can understand the individual qualities of your components, will nearly make you an expert.

Here follow some examples which embody the above principles and procedures. All recipes are for one pound of pasta.

QUICK AND EASY PASTA SAUCES

Garlic and Anchovy Sauce
(Preparation time: 10 minutes)

    2 ozs. butter
    2 ozs. olive oil
    2 cloves garlic
    1 tin anchovies
    chopped parsley

Chop garlic. Mix all ingredients together. Simmer until anchovies dissolve.

Commentary:

Other proportions are acceptable. One of our kids hates anchovies. We, therefore, simmer the garlic in one pot, the anchovies in another. We combine for those who prefer the combination, but serve him garlic sauce only.

Broccoli, Cauliflower and/or Asparagus Sauce
(Preparation time: 20 minutes or less)

> 1 lb. broccoli, or 1 lb. asparagus, or 1 head of cauliflower or
>   a combination of about 1 lb. (altogether) of two or
>   all three thereof
> 2 tbsps. butter
> 2 tbsps. olive oil
> 2 ozs. white wine
> 4 ozs. heavy sweet cream
> ¼ tsp. ground nutmeg
> salt
> pepper

For broccoli: Prepare by cutting flowerlets away from stems so that you end up with a large number of tiny flowerlets. Slice stems very thin into what would be thin discs if stems were cylindrical.

For cauliflower: Cut away green leaves, cut a conical section out of bottom so that flowers fall apart. Cut thicker part of remaining stems away from flowerlets so that you end up with many tiny flowerlets. Slice stems thinly into what would be discs if stems were cylindrical. If large, irregular cross sections result cut into pieces about size of 25 cent and 50 cent pieces.

For asparagus: Cut away and discard about 2″ of bottom. Peel with vegetable peeler within an inch or two of tip. Cut off tips and remainder into 1″ cylinders.

Sauté pieces and/or flowerlets in butter and oil over medium high heat for three minutes, stirring occasionally. Add white wine, return to medium simmer for five minutes. Add sweet cream, bubble at high heat 1–2 minutes stirring to avoid burning until viscous, almost thick. Add nutmeg. Salt and pepper to taste.

Sausage Sauce

(For 1 lb. pasta, preferably one with large tubular or complex shape to which the heavy pieces of the sauce will adhere)
(*Preparation time: 20 minutes or less*)

2 onions
2 cloves garlic
6 tbsps. olive oil
1 lb. sausage (Italian, sweet or hot, breakfast, pepperoni, chorizo, or any other)
¼ cup ground parmesan or other hard cheese (e.g., romano, asiago, raclette)
salt
pepper

Slice onions, chop garlic, sauté in oil until soft. Slice sausage into about ¼–½″ discs. Place in another pan in enough water to cover. Simmer until water evaporates, brown in fat which has run off. Pour away fat. Add sausage to onions and garlic, sauté together 3–4 minutes. Turn off flame, mix thoroughly with cheese. Salt, pepper to taste.

Tomato Sauce
(Preparation time: 45 minutes)

1 lb. tomatoes (canned or fresh, whichever is better. Or you
      may use tomato purée—Pomi is very good)
1 onion
2 cloves garlic
1 carrot
1 piece orange peel
1 tbsp. capers
4 tbsps. olive oil
1 bay leaf
1 tsp. oregano
salt
pepper

Peel and chop onion, peel and slice garlic, peel and slice carrot
thin. Sauté in olive oil until soft. Chop tomato. Add to pot along
with all other ingredients, except capers. Simmer uncovered for
40 minutes or longer until thick. Add capers. Serve over pasta
either unstrained or strained, as you prefer.

Commentary:

This sauce has many variations. The capers and/or orange peel
and/or carrot may be omitted. Anchovies may be added. So may
olives, chopped green pepper and red bell pepper or hot red pepper. Chopped celery and/or parsley may be added. Any fresh herbs
are always welcome. Leeks and/or shallots could be used in place
of onion. Mushrooms could be sliced, sautéed separately and then
added. A cup of red wine is good. It should be added at the outset
so that the simmering reduces it.

We have, however, as our basic sauce presented the simplest
version. Undoubtedly you will want to build on it.

Fettucini Alfredo
(Preparation time: 20 minutes)

A famous dish, not low in calories (you needn't eat to excess!) but delicious and simple. Variations exist. Taste is determined by deftness of preparation and excellence of ingredients.

> **1 lb. fettucini**
> **1 cup heavy sweet cream**
> **¼ lb. butter**
> **2 egg yolks**
> **½–⅔ cup parmesan, asiago, romano or other grated hard, dried cheese**
> **black pepper**
> **pinch of allspice or nutmeg**

In heavy pot large enough to hold cooked fettucini, melt butter, add most of cream, keep warm.

Cook fettucini 2 minutes less than recommended on box: cooking will be completed in warm cream. Drain, add to warm cream, stir for a minute or two, remove from flame, add egg yolks, ⅔ of cheese and balance of cream. Stir together. Return to low flame to heat. Serve immediately. Add balance of cheese and black pepper. Dust allspice or nutmeg on surface. Serve on hot plates.

Mushroom Sauce
(Preparation time: 5–10 minutes)

> 1 lb. mushrooms, quartered, or if large, cut in 6–8 sections
> 2 cloves garlic, sliced
> 2 ozs. oil
> 1 small, or ½ large sweet red pepper, chopped
> salt
> fresh ground pepper
> grated parmesan or other dried cheese

Heat oil, sauté garlic until soft, salt mushrooms, add to oil over very high flame, stir rapidly so that mushrooms do not burn. In a few minutes mushrooms will exude liquid. Add chopped red pepper. Reduce flame. Stir until liquid almost completely evaporates which may take 3–5 minutes. Pour over pasta. Add ground black pepper and cheese.

Sauce Orientale
(Preparation time: 5–10 minutes)

> 2 ozs. sesame oil (olive oil or butter may substitute)
> 2 ozs. soy sauce
> 4 tbsps. peanut butter
> 6 ozs. chicken broth
> 1 oz. currants (raisins may substitute)

Heat oil, add soy sauce, when at a simmer add peanut butter, stir, dissolve. Add currants. This sauce may be served hot over hot spaghetti or linguini or mixed with pasta and served cold. You might try Chinese or Japanese noodles, rice or buckwheat.

Chicken Liver Sauce
(Preparation time: 30–40 minutes)

1 lb. chicken livers
1 onion, chopped
2 cloves garlic, chopped
1 sweet red pepper, chopped
½ cup canned tomatoes
2 tbsps. olive oil
1 bay leaf
1 small bunch parsley, chopped
1 tsp. oregano
2 ozs. sherry
salt
pepper

Trim livers, discarding yellow string-like part. Cut into quarters, e.g., each lobe in half, or as close to that as you can, because sometimes what's a lobe is not entirely clear. Chop onion and garlic. Sauté them in oil until limp. Add livers over high heat until exteriors are browned. Remove liver and set aside. Chop sweet red pepper, parsley and tomato, add to pan with sherry and salt, pepper and herbs. Simmer lightly uncovered 20 minutes or more until thick. Return livers to pan until heated through. Serve.

Pasta Shells with Walnuts or Hazelnuts (or both)
(Preparation time: 15 minutes)

Serves 4–6

6–8 ozs. walnuts or hazelnuts (pecans, cashews, macadamia,
     etc. will do)
2 cloves garlic
6 ozs. olive or vegetable oil (or butter)
1 lb. small pasta shells
6 ozs. grated parmesan or other hard cheese
2 tbsps. salt

Chop garlic, add salt to water, bring water to boil, add shells
to water. Heat oil, add garlic to oil. As it browns, add nuts. Stir.
Nuts should brown but not burn. Be careful—they start burning
very suddenly. When pasta is done *al dente* (check after about half
the cooking time on box has elapsed; if not done, keep checking
every minute or two), drain, pour nuts and oil over pasta, cover
with cheese. Mix. Serve.

Cold Pasta Primavera Debby
(Preparation time: 20 minutes or less)

    1 lb. small pasta shells (cartwheels or other shapes with holes
        and/or declivities will do)
    6 qts. water
    2 tbsps. salt
    10 ozs. tiny frozen peas
    2 carrots
    1 red pepper
    1 pt. cherry tomatoes
    1 head of broccoli
    1 lemon
    4 tbsps. vegetable oil
    1 cup sweet cream or 1 cup yogurt or 1 cup vinaigrette
        (more optional)
    ½ cup grated parmesan cheese

Optional: other vegetables and/or walnuts or hazelnuts

    As pasta water heats, chop carrots and red pepper into about ½" chunks. Cut cherry tomatoes in half. Cut flowerlets from broccoli. Cut broccoli stems into ½" thick disc like slices. Chop optional vegetables, if any. Sauté carrots, pepper and broccoli stems in oil for 3–4 minutes. Allow peas to defrost while pasta water heats and pasta cooks. Remove lemon zest (the yellow coating of the lemon skin), with a carrot peeler or lemon zester or very sharp knife, from lemon and chop into tiny slivers. When pasta is *al dente* (taste when it has cooked half the time recommended on the box; if not done test in another minute or two) pour into colander, add peas and quickly cool under running water. Shake out water remaining in shells. Place in serving bowl. Pour other vegetables (and nuts, if any) over pasta. Add cream, yogurt or vinaigrette. You may add a little more if you prefer. Top with parmesan. Sprinkle lemon zest on top. Toss and serve.

Hot Pasta Primavera Debby
(Preparation time: 20 minutes or less)

1 lb. small shells (or other pasta with holes or declivities)
1 cup grated carrots
1 cup grated zucchini
1 cup yogurt (more optional)
2 tbsps. butter
4 tbsps. salt
6 qts. water
freshly ground pepper

Peel carrots, scrub zucchini. Add 2 tbsps. salt to water. Bring to boil. As water heats grate carrots and zucchini in a food processor or with a hand grater. Place grated carrots and zucchini in a colander. Add remaining 2 tbsps. salt. As water comes to boil add pasta. Remove water from carrots and zucchini (by squeezing in your fist). Melt butter in pan. Gently sauté carrots and zucchini. When pasta is *al dente* (test it first after it has cooked half the time recommended on the box), drain, pour sautéed vegetables over, add yogurt. You may add a bit more if you prefer. Toss. Serve. Add freshly ground pepper.

CHAPTER IX

Vegetables

Vegetables may be prepared in various ways other than simply steaming, broiling or sautéing. They are probably most interesting stuffed. They also have fine appearance and flavor presented vinaigrette. And when prepared alone, a variety of flavorings enhance their natural attractiveness.

COLD COOKED VEGETABLES VINAIGRETTE

Many vegetables lend themselves to quick preparation for serving cold with a vinaigrette sauce. Some, like asparagus, artichoke hearts or bottoms, mushrooms and leeks are often served as a first course. But there is no reason why beets, stringbeans, cauliflower, broccoli or small white potatoes can't be first course material, although usually they aren't accorded that stature.

A combination of several, assembled for color and complementarity of flavor makes a beautiful platter to serve as first course or accompaniment. Bright red beets, bright green stringbeans, broccoli and/or orange carrots assembled alternately with pale cauliflower, potato and/or mushrooms make a striking presentation.

It is better to undercook vegetables slightly, to be eaten crisp. Vinaigretting softens them further. Suggested cooking times should produce that result. Pour the sauce over the vegetables while they are hot, facilitating absorption of flavor.

Artichoke Bottoms. Bend back the leaves and pull off until all that remains is the silky inner cone. Cutting with the knife point gently into the base of the cone, where the leaves emerge from the bottom, separate the remaining silky leaves from the bottom, which, unless you have cut at precisely the right level, will be covered by the furry choke. Trim away the fur. Trim away from the base the green stubs of the larger leaves. Immediately cover the bottom with oil or lemon juice to prevent discoloration. For tenderness, large artichoke bottoms should be cooked 12–15 minutes, small ones less. Some may consider this undercooked but we prefer crispness. Of course, you may cook longer. Pour vinaigrette sauce over. Serve at room temperature or cold, either as soon as cooked or within the next day or two.

Asparagus. Cut off tough ends, perhaps an inch or so. Scrape away outer fibers with vegetable peeler, up towards the tip where the asparagus is tender. Boil a large amount of water—so that when the asparagus is dropped in it will return to a boil quickly, minimizing cooking time. We don't tie them up in a bunch, as recommended by some fanatics. It seems not worth the trouble. The only advantages we can see in binding is that they are easier to fish out, the tips are less likely to break off and there is a certain fetishistic satisfaction in the process. If you find that binding serves any of these purposes go ahead. When they come to a boil, cook three minutes for very thin ones, five minutes for heavy specimens. The aim is to have a crisp asparagus and you may adjust cooking time to your taste. They are delicious raw, so don't fear undercooking. After extracting, pour vinaigrette over. Serve either as soon as cool or cold, as promptly as convenient.

Commentary:

The length of this disquisition tells something about how asparagus enlists passions. Their preparation reminds us of other procedures which evoke controversy over what—in the cosmic scheme—is of slight importance: waterproofing boots, breaking in pipes, opening and pouring wine. Some asparagus experts advise steaming rather than boiling or vice versa, binding together for cooking or tossing into the pot loose, cooking standing up or lying down, using certain kinds of pots, quantities of water and so forth. Most—not all—seem to agree about the importance of cutting away tough fibers.

Beets. The best beet advice we've seen is: cut away stems, allowing an inch to protrude. Wrap tightly in aluminum foil. Place in 425 degree oven 30 minutes to an hour depending on size of beets. For only a few beets we use the toaster oven. Cool under running water. Trim, peel, slice thin. Pour vinaigrette over. Serve cool or cold when convenient.

Broccoli. Cut off heavy stems, just below where they diverge into smaller branches. Break into flowerlets. Plunge into rapidly boiling unsalted water. Boil three minutes. Pour vinaigrette over. Serve cool or cold when convenient.

Commentary:

Louis P. DeGouy is one of the few writers who waxes precious on the subject of broccoli: "After the well-known fact that asparagus should be cooked standing up, comes the reminder that broccoli should be handled the same way. When broccoli is cooked 'on its feet' there is less breaking off of the tender top buds and they are not 'cooked to pieces'." What can anyone say? It does cook more quickly, however, when first broken into flowerlets and, if cooked *al dente,* is unlikely to deteriorate in the process.

Carrots. Tiny ones need not be peeled; larger ones should be peeled, quartered, the wood-like core sliced away, then cut into two inch sticks. Boil eight minutes. Pour vinaigrette over. Serve as soon as cool or cold when convenient. Stir fry in a bit of brown sugar and rum, brandy or bourbon instead of vinaigrette if you like.

Cauliflower. Break into flowerlets. Boil 3 minutes. Remove from water. Pour vinaigrette over and serve cool or cold when convenient.

Leeks. Cut off roots and all but a couple of inches of green leaves. Clean very very thoroughly by cutting slits in ends, rinsing, shaking under water, and otherwise carefully extracting sand, which clings doggedly. Simmer ten minutes for medium size, more or less for other sizes. Remove. Pour vinaigrette over. Serve cool or cold when convenient.

Commentary:

We think leeks are the most underutilized vegetable in American cuisine. They look terrific and taste delicious alone or as part of a complex preparation. Maybe their rarity makes them classy. Anyway, an appetizer of leeks vinaigrette or otherwise prepared (see below) is impressive.

Other technique: Place in pan, add 1 cup red wine, 1 cup beef broth (from cubes if most convenient), 1 bay leaf. Simmer 15–20 minutes. They may be rubbed with olive oil and grilled, too. Ten to twelve minutes. Watch to prevent burning.

Mushrooms. Trim stems, wash, put in boiling water two minutes. Remove. Pour vinaigrette over. Serve cool or cold when convenient. Or, slice, salt, sauté in oil until liquid is thrown off. Reduce flame until liquid nearly evaporates.

Onions. Boil small golf ball size white onions in skins 15 minutes. Remove from water. Rinse in cold water. Remove skins (a process which doesn't even require a knife, since boiling has done most of the work). Pour vinaigrette over. Serve cool or cold when convenient.

Potatoes. Use small golf ball size potatoes. Boil 18 minutes. Rinse in cold water. Peel. (You may not even need a knife since boiling has done most of the job). Slice thin. Pour vinaigrette over. Serve cool or cold when convenient. Another option: After slicing you may sauté in previously sautéed, chopped onion and garlic for a few minutes.

Stringbeans. The thinner the better. Trim ends. Cut into two inch pieces, or if you like the looks of long slender ones, don't. Boil 6 minutes. Remove. Pour vinaigrette over. Serve cool or cold when convenient.

Zucchini. Cut into quarters and then into two inch segments. Boil 2–3 minutes. Remove. Pour vinaigrette over. Serve cool or cold when convenient.

Vinaigrette (for cold vegetables)
(Preparation time: 5 minutes)

    3 ozs. olive oil
    1 oz. vinegar
    1 tbsp. finely chopped onion
    1 tbsp. capers
    chopped fresh herbs (or pinch of rosemary, thyme, tarragon,
          etc.) if available
    salt
    pepper

Commentary:

See also the Vinaigrette for Salads, p. 47.

One might vary the ingredients to suit what the sauce will flavor. E.g., perhaps less vinegar for vegetables with unique delicate flavor, like asparagus or artichoke. Perhaps a bit more vinegar and capers or onion for blander boiled potatoes.

Color can be important: chopped egg whites for the darker greens or beets; dark green capers for white cauliflower, potatoes, and so forth.

If you don't think it too complicated and productive of more dirty dishes than you can stand, set out dishes of all or most of the potential ingredients, oil, vinegar and lemon juice so that everyone at the table can mix their own.

OTHER VEGETABLE PREPARATION

TOPPINGS

Garlic and Oil Sauté. Heat two tablespoons oil, add two cloves garlic, sliced. Brown the garlic. Add either broccoli, cauliflower, carrots, leeks, mushrooms, potatoes, spinach, stringbeans, zucchini, after having been prepared as above. Stir in hot oil until browned. Serve hot.

Wine and Herbs Sauté. Heat two tablespoons oil, brown either leeks or onions after having been prepared as above. Add two ounces cream sherry or other sweet fortified wine, two tablespoons lemon juice, bay leaf (or other herb) one teaspoon sugar, salt, pepper. Cool until liquid reduces to a couple of tablespoons. Remove, pour liquid over. Serve hot or cold.

Grand Marnier. Heat two tablespoons oil. Brown in it carrots as prepared above. Reduce flame to minimum. Add four tablespoons Grand Marnier, one pat butter. Simmer for 2 minutes. Serve.

Buttered Crumbs. Melt half a stick or more of butter. Add 3–4 tablespoons of breadcrumbs, stir thoroughly until somewhat brown. Spoon over asparagus, broccoli, cauliflower, zucchini. Serve hot.

STUFFED VEGETABLES
(Preparation and cooking time: 30–50 minutes depending on vegetable being prepared and stuffing)

Serves 4–6

Introductory:

Stuffed vegetables make a beautiful presentation, green, red, white, the stuffings golden or brown. One easily can make an hors d'oeuvres tray of assorted stuffed vegetables that will equal or surpass what is found in many good French, Italian, or Greek restaurants. A simple dinner achieves a certain elegance preceded or accompanied by colorful and delicious stuffed tomatoes, zucchini and so forth. Stuffed artichokes are sometimes served as a main course; tomato, zucchini, red and green peppers, and onions could be the centerpiece of any meal. Quantities suggested in the following recipes are for appetizers or side dishes. Greater quantities, of course, should be used for main courses.

The general approach to preparation for all such dishes is the same. Basically, the harder vegetables, e.g., onions, zucchini, peppers, artichokes, should be precooked to make them tender before stuffing. Since time is of the essence, the stuffings should be prepared while precooking is going on. Tomatoes and mushroom caps first may be browned in butter for appearance and flavor. After stuffing, the vegetable should be baked to finish the process, except for the artichokes, which become tender more quickly by steaming. They should be stood up in an inch of water in a large pot.

The stuffings presented here can be varied endlessly. See suggestions following the recipes.

First presented are three basic stuffings. Then follows preparation of the vegetables and the final cooking together.

STUFFINGS
(These can be largely or entirely prepared
while vegetables are precooking)

Anchovies and Breadcrumbs
(Stuffing No. 1)
(Preparation time: 15 minutes)

    3 tbsps. oil (olive or vegetable)
    1 tbsp. garlic
    1 large onion
    ¼ tsp. oregano
    ¼ tsp. thyme
    ¼ tsp. tarragon
    1 tbsp. chopped parsley
    1 tbsp. chopped anchovies (first marinated in vinegar
            10 minutes)
    1 cup bread crumbs
    ¼ cup grated parmesan or grated cheese (e.g. asiago, romano,
            swiss, Jarlsberg)
    fresh ground pepper

Heat oil in a medium saucepan. Chop garlic. Over medium flame add garlic and stir a bit until it begins to brown. Chop and add onion. Cook at medium heat five minutes. Add herbs and anchovies. Stir. Add bread crumbs. Mix thoroughly. If dry, add a tbsp. or two more of oil. Turn off flame. Allow to cool for a minute or two. Add parmesan or other cheese. (If you add cheese while cooking, it will stick to pan.) Season with pepper. No salt needed; the anchovies supply enough. Yield: 1 cup (plus) stuffing.

Ground Meat Stuffing
(Stuffing No. 2)
(Preparation time: 15 minutes)

2 tbsps. butter
2 strips bacon, finely chopped
1½ tbsps. chopped garlic
½ cup chopped onion
½ lb. ground meat (hamburger, pork or any other meat or combination thereof)
¼ cup grated parmesan or other cheese (e.g., swiss, asiago, romano, Jarlsberg)

Melt butter in pan. Heat bacon in melted butter until fat melts. Add garlic. When it begins to brown, add onion. Sauté 3–4 minutes until onions become soft. Add ground meat. Cook over medium flame 5 minutes. Pour off excess fat. Add herbs. Add bread crumbs. If mixture is dry, add a tbsp. or 2 more oil. Mix again thoroughly. Turn off flame. Allow to cool for a minute or two. Add cheese. (Again, if added while flame is on, cheese will stick to pan). Stir thoroughly. Yield: about 1½ cups.

Cheese Stuffing
(Stuffing No. 3)
(Preparation time: 15 minutes)

½ lb. swiss, gruyere, Jarlsberg, or emmenthaler cheese
3 ozs. white wine
1 tbsp. Dijon or other hot prepared mustard
1 clove garlic, finely chopped or crushed white pepper

Chop cheese into small chunks, place in double boiler or sauce-pan on a flametamer, medium flame, until cheese starts melting. Add remaining ingredients, mix thoroughly, until cheese is all melted. (This stuffing must be poured into vegetable while hot.) Sprinkle a bit of paprika on the stuffing after it has been poured into the vegetables. It enhances the browning.

Other Stuffings

Other stuffings may be made from instant ceviche (drained of its liquid) see p. 17 and instant shrimp hash, see p. 26, supra.

PREPARING, STUFFING, COOKING VEGETABLES

Onions. Take 4–6 medium onions; peel, cut off top, about ⅓ way down. Place in boiling water for 10 minutes. Remove and cool under running water. With spoon or grapefruit knife, scoop out inner shells leaving two or three layers of outer shell. (You may reserve scooped out interior to be used in other dishes, including stuffing). Fill with stuffing 1, 2 or 3. Place on oiled pan, cover with aluminum foil or otherwise, and bake 15 minutes in oven preheated to 350 degrees. With stuffing 1 or 2, sprinkle some grated parmesan on top before baking. Place under broiler for a minute or two before serving. Stuffing 1 or 2 can be served hot or cold or next day. With 3, the vegetables should be served hot.

Zucchini. Select enough zucchini to hold the amount of stuffing you are making. Approximately two large zucchini (typical cucumber size) will hold one recipe of each of the suggested stuffing. Scrub to remove sand which often is found in skin. Place in boiling water 3–4 minutes. Remove. Cool under running water. Cut off ends. Cut into 1½″ cylinders. With spoon or grapefruit knife, scoop out, leaving walls and bottom of ¼–½″ thickness. Alternatively, cut lengthwise, forming two boat shaped pieces, sort of dugout canoes. (The residual scooped out zucchini may be chopped and sautéed with onions, etc. of stuffings 1 or 2). Add stuffing 1, 2 or 3. With 1 or 2, sprinkle a bit of parmesan on top before baking. Cover with aluminum foil, or wax paper, bake 15 minutes in oven preheated to 350 degrees. Place under broiler a minute or two before serving. Stuffing 1 or 2 can be served hot or cold or even the next day. With stuffing 3, should be served hot.

Artichokes. Take 4–6 artichokes (medium size); tear off tough outer leaves around base. With knife or scissors, cut tops of leaves off across top. Cut remaining sharp points off remaining leaves on which they still remain. A pair of scissors is best for this. Place upside down on counter and force downward gently, causing leaves to spread. Don't press too hard or artichoke will split. With grape-fruit knife or other suitable implement (e.g., a melon ball scoop), scrape out hairy choke. Place in water to boil 20 minutes. Cool under running water. Add stuffing 1 or 2 o center and, if there is enough, also among the leaves. Place in pot with about an inch of water. Cover. Bring water to boil. Allow to steam 20 minutes more. Can be served hot or cold. If hot, serve with melted butter. If cold, with a vinaigrette sauce.

Commentary:

The artichoke is eaten by tearing off the leaves, dipping in butter or vinaigrette and, between your front teeth, scraping flesh off leaves. Bits of stuffing cling to the leaves enhancing this flavor. The bottom and stuffing are delicious when eaten together.

Peppers. Take 4–6 medium red, green and/or yellow peppers or 8–12 small hot (picante) red or green cherry peppers (a combi-nation of colors and piquancy is interesting and colorful). Yellow peppers, which occasionally are available, enhance the appearance. Make a small slit in each pepper to prevent bursting while boiling; place in boiling water 10 minutes. Cool under running water. Cut off tops (save them) and clean out seeds and veins. A few remaining seeds are not terrible. Spoon stuffing 1 or 2 into peppers. Replace tops on peppers. Place in oiled baking dish, cover with aluminum foil or otherwise and place for 15 minutes in preheated 350 degree oven. Can be served hot or cold.

Tomatoes. Take 4–6 medium to large tomatoes; with grapefruit knife, scoop out, leaving wall up to ½" thick; remove seeds. No precooking necessary. Add stuffing 1, 2 or 3. Place in oiled baking dish, cover with aluminum foil or otherwise, bake in preheated oven 15 minutes at 350 degrees. Can be served hot or cold, but if using stuffing 3, serve hot. Place under broiler to brown before serving. You may save scooped out tomato to make tomato sauce.

Mushrooms. Take 8–12 large mushrooms, the larger the better. Remove stems which you may chop and use in some other dish, or sauté and use as part of the stuffing for the mushrooms. Place in oiled baking dish, cover with aluminum foil or otherwise, bake in oven preheated to 350 degrees for 15 minutes. Before serving, place under broiler a few minutes to brown. May be served hot or cold, but if using stuffing 3, heat before serving.

Commentary:

Once ingredients are assembled, each of the stuffings takes perhaps 10 minutes to make. Vegetable preparation is simple. Artichokes, and to a lesser extent peppers, present minor difficulties. The second time you prepare them, they should be a breeze. Fresh herbs, any of them, are preferable to dry herbs. Other herbs, if available, may be used in addition to or in place of those in the recipes. If you have no dried bread crumbs, you can make them fresh by tossing a few slices of bread into the blender or food processor, or you may use cooked rice in lieu of breadcrumbs. Converted rice is relatively quick to make. After it has been cooked, mix it into the recipe as you would the bread crumbs. Lentils, which have been precooked according to instructions on the box, also may be used instead of bread crumbs.

Here are a few additional vegetable dishes simpler than those presented above:

Spinach
(Preparation and cooking time: 10 minutes)

Serves 4–6

> 1 lb. spinach
> 2 cloves garlic sliced
> 4 tbsps. olive oil
> salt, pepper

Wash spinach exceedingly thoroughly to remove all sand. Place in boiling water to cover for three to five minutes. Squeeze dry. Sauté garlic in oil until nearly brown. Place spinach in pan, stir two to three minutes. Salt and pepper to taste. Serve.

Commentary:

Spinach is arguably the exception to the rule that fresh vegetables are best cooked least. Nevertheless we cook it only briefly. Brillat Savarin presents one recipe in which spinach cooks for more than a day (not a good choice for this book) and M.F.K. Fisher who is nearly infallible, endorses it.

Eggplant and Garlic
(Preparation time: 20 minutes; 5 minutes cooking time)

Serves 4–6

> 2 eggplants
> 4–5 cloves garlic
> 2 scallions
> Pepperoni or chinese sausage
> 2 tbsps. chopped ginger
> ½ cup soy sauce
> 2 tbsps. sugar
> ½ cup peanut oil or vegetable oil

Cut sausage into ½" slices. Fry in oil until brown. Pour off fat. Place in bowl. Add soy sauce, sugar, chopped scallion and chopped ginger. Mix well.

Heat oil in wok or pan. Add garlic, stir for 1 minute. Chop eggplant into 1" cubes. Add eggplant. Stir until all eggplant is covered and absorbs some oil and becomes soft. Add more oil if necessary. Add sausage mixture to eggplant and serve hot.

Endives aux Champignons
(Preparation time: 50–60 minutes; including 30 minutes cooking endives, 10–20 minutes browning)

Serves 6

2 pounds endives
4 oz. fresh mushrooms
1½ oz. butter
½ pint Bechamel sauce (2 oz. butter, 1 oz. flour, 1 pint milk)
4 oz. grated Gruyere cheese

Boil endives 30 minutes in water with a large slice of lemon and a crust of bread to keep endives white. Slice mushrooms and sauté in almost all the butter. Prepare Bechamel sauce and add mushrooms to it. After squeezing all water from endives, put them in an oven serving dish and cover with the Bechamel sauce. Sprinkle cheese and the remaining butter over it. Brown in oven at 400 for 10–20 minutes.

Commentary:

One of a number of doable recipes from a Sabbatical, in England, this one the work of Marina Jarman, an outstanding cook.

Vegetable and Fruit Purées
(Preparation time: 10–15 minutes; 10–15 minutes cooking time)

Serves 4–6

> 6 cups chopped carrot or peas or parsnip (other vegetables
>   may be used)
> ½ stick butter
> 3–4 peaches or apples or pears peeled and chopped
> 1 tbsp. dry sherry or scotch
> ½ cup sour cream
> ¼ tsp. ground nutmeg

Cover vegetables with water and bring to a boil. Reduce heat and simmer until tender. Drain. Meanwhile melt the butter and sauté the fruit for 5 minutes. Add the sherry or scotch and cook for 15 minutes.

Process the vegetables and fruit in a food processor until smooth. Add the nutmeg, sour cream and salt and pepper if needed.

Commentary:

We first had vegetable purées (apart from the baby food we shoved into our children's mouths) at the Paris restaurant, Taillevent, where lamb was served with a trio of purées. If you have a food processor and a microwave oven, they're a cinch. Without the microwave, making the purées ahead and reheating them becomes a problem but not an insurmountable one. And you can time the purée to be ready just in time to serve it.

CHAPTER X

Brunches

Mexican Omelet
(Preparation time: 10–15 minutes; 10–15 minutes cooking time)

Serves 4–6

1 onion
1 tomato
2 cloves garlic
½ lb. Monterey Jack cheese (or Jarlsberg or Swiss)
1 green pepper
1 Jalapeño pepper or 3–4 drops tabasco
6 eggs
6 ozs. oil

Peel, chop onion. Peel, mince garlic, chop tomato and seed, chop green pepper. Sauté all of the above in oil 10–15 minutes over low flame until pepper becomes a bit soft. Beat eggs; add eggs to pan and stir gently until egg curdles. Add chunks of cheese, continue cooking until it melts. Serve.

Cheese, Tomato and Sour Cream Omelet
(Preparation time: 10 minutes; 10 minutes cooking time)

Serves 4–6

3 tbsps. sour cream
2 tbsps. parmesan cheese, freshly grated
¼ tsp. dill powder (optional)
½ tsp. salt
pinch freshly ground pepper
2 large or 3 medium tomatoes, sliced
3 4″ x 7″ slices of Swiss cheese
2 ozs. camembert
1 tbsp. butter
6 eggs

Aggressively beat together the eggs, sour cream, parmesan cheese, dill, salt and pepper. Melt butter in 9″ skillet. Cover bottom of skillet with sliced tomatoes, then cover them with the Swiss cheese. Dot with the camembert. Cook covered over low to medium heat until Swiss cheese is mostly melted. Add egg mixture and sprinkle green pepper on top. Cover and cook over low to medium heat until egg mixture is firm. In covering, allow some room for mixture to rise.

Cut in wedge shaped pieces and serve immediately with dabs of sour cream on top (optional).

Commentary:

This omelet (also known as the Sander omelet after its creator Professor Frank E.A. Sander, Harvard Law School) may be presented in many variations. For the chopped green pepper, one may substitute mushrooms, anchovies, strips of salami or ham—one or more. In lieu of the Swiss cheese, muenster, mozzarella or provolone may be used; for the camembert, brie or other favorite cheese can be substituted—or you can use just one kind of cheese.

Bulka I Pieczarki
(Preparation time: 15 minutes)

Serves 4

1 lb. mushrooms
1 cup onions
4 ozs. butter
4 hard oval breakfast rolls
salt to taste

Slice mushrooms, peel and chop onions, add salt, place in pan, sauté mushroom-onion mixture in pan until onions are soft and mushrooms brown. Using knife handle, poke a hole into rolls, the length of roll. Stuff with mushroom-onion mixture. Serve.

Commentary:

This preparation, sold on the streets of Warsaw by former hot dog vendors, is a substitute for sausages on roll which are no longer available because of the meat shortage there. It is far superior in flavor to hot dogs.

Granny's Blueberry Muffins
(Preparation time: 10 minutes, 30–35 minutes cooking time)

Serves 6

1 level tbsp. butter
Scant ½ cup sugar
1 cup flour
2 tsp. baking powder
½ cup milk
½ cup blueberries rolled in a little of the flour taken from the cup

Cream butter and sugar. Sift flour with baking powder and add to butter-sugar mixture alternately with milk. Fold in berries.

Grease muffin tin and fill each muffin space about three-fourths full. Bake in 350 degree oven for 30–35 minutes. Makes 6 big muffins.

Commentary:

These are so good that we usually double or triple the recipe. If you make them ahead of time, reheat before serving until they feel crunchy on the outside.

Popovers
(Preparation time: 10 minutes; 30 minutes cooking time)

Serves 6

**2 eggs
1 cup milk
1 cup flour
½ tsp. salt**

Put all ingredients in a jar and shake hard. Disregard lumps. Grease and flour muffin tin or special popover tin and fill three-fourths full. Put in a cold oven, turn to 450 degrees, and bake 30 minutes. Check to see if they're done but don't open the oven before the 30 minutes are up. Makes 6 popovers.

CHAPTER XI

Desserts

At the outset of this chapter we acknowledge one premise in addition to those set out in the opening chapter: we doubt that first rate pastry desserts can be prepared from scratch in the time we are assuming will be available. This does not seem to be a serious loss, however. Both of us question the wisdom or pleasure of adding an enormously rich and filling dessert to an unusually splendid dinner. And both believe that one should serve (or eat) very rich desserts only rarely and that their preparation may, without loss of day-to-day pleasure, be left to the first rate pastry chef at your favorite patisserie or restaurant. Pastry for dessert, only when you go out, allows something special to look forward to. Or, as makes good sense, and is possible even at some fine establishments, one may, if it is convenient, leave the home and repair to a nearby resturant for dessert and coffee only.

Fruit of the season and cheese (or either alone) if carefully and imaginatively selected may be the best bet on many occasions. Once a week or so, each of us visits our local cheese shop and orders a few old favorites—a chevre, brie, caerphilly, taleggio, stilton, for example—plus, always, one cheese we have never served before. If you have not already had too much wine, or if there are no activities planned for later in the evening that call for an alert mind and body, a little dessert wine, e.g., a sauternes, tokay, Johannesberg, riesling, or port might be in order.

What we offer here, however, are a few elegant, lively and refreshing desserts, most of which can be prepared within the one hour allotted, and which will not overwhelm a fine meal (or its partakers).

The reader will not be surprised that we put rather heavy emphasis on fruit desserts. We have included a few pastry-mousse-meringue entries that we have found manageable within an hour.

Apple Tart (or Blueberry, Peach, etc.)
(Preparation time: 1 hour; 15 minutes cooking time)

Serves 4–6

½ cup soft butter
¾ cup sugar
2 eggs
grated rind of 1 lemon
4 tsps. lemon juice
1 cup flour
1 tsp. baking powder
1 tsp. salt
5 tart cooking apples peeled and cut into ⅛" slices
2 tbsps. melted butter
1 cup heavy cream whipped
cinnamon

In mixing bowl beat together butter and ½ cup sugar until thoroughly creamed and light. Add eggs one at a time and beat in thoroughly. Beat in lemon rind and 1 tsp. of the juice. Sift together flour, baking powder and salt and gradually add to batter, and beat thoroughly. Turn batter into a buttered 9" springform pan.

Toss apples (or 1½ pints blueberries) with remaining 3 tsps. lemon juice and arrange evenly over batter. Drizzle melted butter over apples; sprinkle with ¼ cup sugar and cinnamon. Bake at 350 degrees for 1 hour or until apples are golden brown and cake pulls away from pan.

Serve while still warm or when cooled. Top with whipped cream (unsweetened or just slightly sweetened) or ice cream.

Macedoine of Fruits
(Preparation time: 15 minutes)

Select fresh ripe fruits of the season. Any combination will do. Cut seedless grapes in half. Seed grapes that have seeds. Hull strawberries, cut in half. Cut apples, pears, peaches into ½″ cubes (first peeling, if you prefer). Slice bananas. Section tangerines. Or use canned mandarin oranges. Papaya or mango chunks would be terrific. Sprinkle with confectioner's sugar. Add a few slices of fresh, or sprinkle of powdered, ginger. Add an ounce or two of orange or lime juice or both. Add two or more ounces of cointreau or triple sec. Douse liberally with white wine or, if you feel expansive, champagne. Chill, serve.

Poached Peaches with Raspberry Sauce
(Preparation and cooking time: 20 minutes)

Serves 4

4 peaches (6, if small)
1 cup water
½ cup sugar
¼ lemon
1 pkg. frozen raspberries

(If you are not using raspberries, make it one cup sugar and one tsp. vanilla extract or one inch of vanilla bean and ½ cup burgundy or other red wine.)

Place peaches in a saucepan of boiling water for 2 minutes; remove and douse with cold water and peel. You should be able to scrape skin off easily with fork, knife and fingers. Bring cup of water, sugar and lemon to a boil, add peeled peaches and boil lightly for 4 minutes. Drain and refrigerate peaches.

Strain defrosted raspberries, process for a few seconds, and serve with whole peaches.

Follow same recipe for fresh, ripe pears, except they should be cut in half and core removed; kept in cold water until ready to cook; and poached for 15 minutes instead of 5.

Commentary:

This dessert is outstanding for the period of the year when fresh peaches are available. We have experimented with it on high-quality home-preserved peaches and it is very good and indeed may be a reason for putting up peaches. Not even the raspberry sauce keeps canned peaches from tasting like canned peaches but if you are resolved to serve canned peaches, the sauce helps a lot.

Orange Slices with Red Wine Sauce
(Preparation time: 15 minutes)

Serves 4–6

> 4–6 seedless eating oranges, depending on size and appetites
> 1 tbsp. grated orange rind
> 1 cup red wine (Bordeaux or Burgundy)
> ⅓ cup sugar
> ½″ cinnamon stick
> 1 slice lemon, seeded
> 2 sectioned tangerines (if easily available)

Peel and slice oranges and arrange in separate dishes. Boil wine, rind, sugar, lemon slice, tangerine and cinnamon stick (a few shakes of powdered cinnamon may be substituted) 5 minutes. Remove stick and pour over oranges. Serve cold.

Commentary:

This is light, refreshing, and has a particularly high elegance/labor ratio.

Oranges Givres
(Preparation time: 15 minutes)

Serves 4

4 large attractive oranges
1 pt. orange, lemon or lime sherbet
8 tbsps. Grand Marnier liqueur

Cut top off oranges, about ¼ way below top. Remove flesh with a grapefruit knife being careful not to damage peel. Allow sherbet to stand perhaps 10 minutes at room temperature and become somewhat soft. Mix the Grand Marnier and a little of the orange pulp with the sherbet and fill the orange shells. Place in freezer ½ hour or more and serve, making sure the sherbet is soft enough to be scooped out without great effort—or else the shell may go skittering off the table.

Commentary:

Other flavors, other liqueurs, vodka or rum may be used with filling. If orange has been in freezer long enough to become very hard, remove long enough before serving (perhaps 20 minutes) to allow sherbet to soften somewhat before serving. This dish may be made with lemons or limes (large ones are better) or melon (small ones are better).

Broiled Grapefruit or Orange
(Preparation time: 20 minutes)

Grapefruit halves or large navel orange halves at room
         temperature
2 tsps. sugar per grapefruit; 1 tsp. sugar per orange half
¼ tsp. powdered nutmeg
¼ tsp. powdered cinnamon
¼ tsp. powdered allspice
¼ tsp. cloves
2 tbsps. liqueur (Grand Marnier, Kirsch, cognac) or dark rum
         per grapefruit half or 1 tbsp. per orange half
1 pat butter per grapefruit half; ½ pat butter per orange half

Section grapefruit or orange with a grapefruit knife. Mix sugar
and spices and sprinkle on fruit (2 tbsps. per grapefruit; 1 tbsp.
per orange). Pour liqueur on fruit (2 tbsps. per grapefruit; 2 tbsp.
per orange). Dice pats of butter and dot fruit with it (1 pat per
grapefruit; ½ pat per orange). Preheat broiler. Place fruit in flame
proof dish under broiler 6 or 7 minutes, until browned. Serve,
preferably, hot or at room temperature.

Commentary:

If the fruit is not at room temperature when placed under
broiler it will emerge hot on top and chilled below. Not terrible.
If, however, you want it heated through and the fruit is cold you
may place in a warm oven for five minutes before topping with
sugar, etc. If you place in oven to warm, add sugar-spice mixture,
butter, liqueur afterward and before broiling. Otherwise what you
add will dissolve before broiling and no brown crust will form.

Chocolate Meringue Ring
(Preparation time: 1 hour 20 minutes)

Serves 6–8

5 egg whites
1¼ cup granulated sugar
2 tbsps. unsweetened cocoa
½ pt. whipping cream

Beat egg whites stiff. Sift and mix sugar with cocoa and mix slowly into egg whites. Place in a greased 6-cup ring mold and cook in 225 degree oven for one hour with the mold resting in a pan of water. After removing from oven, let mold stand for 10 minutes and turn upside-down on a serving dish. Whip cream, adding (optionally) 3 tbsps. cognac, Grand Marnier or sherry and pile whipped cream in center of ring.

Commentary:

This dessert is elegant and sweet without being overwhelmingly rich and complex. It has the further advantage that there practically is nothing that can go wrong in the preparation (a challenge about which we will probably hear from our readers).

Strawberries Romanoff
(Preparation time: 10 minutes)

Serves 4–6

2 qts. fresh strawberries
½ cup sugar
1 pt. vanilla ice cream
½ pt. whipping cream
½ cup cointreau

Hull and sugar strawberries. Whip cream and fold in ice cream. Add cointreau, mix with strawberries and serve immediately.

Apple and/or Plum Crisp
(Preparation time: 15 minutes; 30 minutes baking time)

Serves 4–6

4 cups sliced Macintosh apples (golden delicious are firmer but have less flavor)
½ lemon
⅔ cup brown sugar packed
¾ cup flour
¾ cup oats
¾ tsp. cinnamon
¾ tsp. nutmeg
7 tbsps. softened butter

Grease an 8″ or 9″ pan. Arrange sliced apples in bottom of pan and sprinkle with lemon juice. Mix remaining ingredients until they are crumb-like and sprinkle over apples. Bake at 375 degrees for 30 minutes or until brown.

Commentary:

Variations: (1) Small purple Italian plums may be substituted for apples or may be combined with apples in alternating rows. (2) One of us likes to add a thin layer of granola over the top. (3) Whipped cream with or without a sherry or brandy flavoring may be added.

Mocha Mousse
(Preparation and cooking time: 20 minutes)

Serves 8

3 squares unsweetened chocolate
½ cup water
¾ cup sugar
⅛ tsp. salt
3 egg yolks
1 tbsp. instant coffee
1 tbsp. vanilla
2 cups heavy cream, whipped

Bring chocolate and water to a boil over low heat. Stir until blended. Stir in sugar and cook for three minutes. Beat egg yolks and stir them in, followed by coffee. (If you have only freeze-dried coffee, dissolve it in a bit of hot water before adding.) Whip cream with vanilla and fold it in. Refrigerate in the serving bowl until firm. If the mousse does not become firm in 10–15 minutes, place it in the freezer for a few minutes before serving.

Cream Mold
(Preparation and cooking time: 20 minutes)

Serves 6–8

1 envelope plain gelatin
¾ cup sugar
1 cup heavy cream
1 cup light cream
1 tsp. vanilla
2 cups sour cream
1 pkg. frozen raspberries (or strawberries)

Mix gelatin and sugar. Stir in heavy and light cream. Let sit for 5 minutes. Put on low heat and stir until gelatin is dissolved. Take off heat and cool until lukewarm. Add vanilla and sour cream. Mix until smooth. Pour into 6 cup mold. Refrigerate or freeze until chilled but not frozen. Serve with frozen berries.

Lemon Angel Pie
(Preparation time: for shell 5 minutes; 1½ hours baking time; 15 minutes filling preparation time)

Serves 6

Meringue:

> **4 egg whites**
> **1 cup sugar**
> **pinch of cream of tartar**

Beat egg whites, add sugar and cream of tartar, and continue beating (electric mixers help) until meringue is stiff. Arrange in a 10″ greased pyrex pie plate as a shell and bake at 250 degrees for 1½ hours. Let cool in oven after you turn it off.

Filling:

> **4 egg yolks**
> **½ cup sugar**
> **pinch of salt**
> **6 tbsp. fresh lemon juice**
> **½ pint (or a little more) heavy cream**

Mix together all ingredients except cream. Cook in a heavy pan, stirring continuously with a wooden spoon, until thick. Cook still stirring another 5 minutes. Beat vigorously and cool. Whip cream and fold into cooled egg-lemon mixture. Fill meringue shell and refrigerate at least two hours.

Commentary:

This is the Vorenbergs' all-time favorite dessert and is always a hit. It does not meet the one hour standard but very well meets the lightness factor described earlier. However, for working people, all you have to do is make the meringue shell the night before and leave in the oven (turned off of course). In the morning you can quickly make the filling (10–15 minutes) and leave the pie in the fridge all day.

Oranges Fez
(Preparation time: 5–10 minutes)

Serves 4

4 chilled oranges (navel are preferable)
4 tsps. sugar
2 tsps. cinnamon powder

Chill oranges, peel, slice into half inch slices. Sprinkle sugar on slices. Then sprinkle cinnamon. Chill for at least 10 minutes. Serve.

Commentary:

The simplest, yet most refreshing of desserts which is from— obvious as it might seem—Fez, Morocco.

Gorgonzola and Honey
(Preparation time: 1–2 minutes)

8–12 ozs. soft gorgonzola cheese (other blue cheeses,
   e.g. stilton, roquefort will do)
8–12 ozs. honey
Well baked French or Italian bread (sourdough preferable)

Cheese should be at room temperature. Serve each diner a
slice and dribble honey over. Eat with bread.

Commentary:

There are times when the Greenbergs think this is the best
dessert they ever had.

Citrus Mousse
(Preparation time: 30 minutes)

Serves 8

3 eggs separated
¼ cup sugar plus ½ tbsp.
¼ cup boiling water
½ cup lime, lemon or orange juice
1 tbsp. grated rind of fruit
½ tbsp. gelatin
1 cup heavy cream
pinch of salt

Combine citrus juice with gelatin. Set aside. Wisk cream and
rind to medium firm peaks. Chill. Beat yolks with ¼ cup sugar
until very pale yellow. Wisk in boiling water until frothy. Set over
double boiler and cook over low heat, stirring constantly with rub-

ber spatula until mixture holds a firm straight line on spatula. Heat citrus juice and gelatin until warm and add to egg yolk mixture, beating until cool. Fold into whipped cream. Beat egg white with salt and ½ tbsp. sugar to medium firm peaks and fold into whipped cream mixture. This needs two hours of chilling before serving.

Note: Our favorite flavor is lime. For a glamorous dessert, the mousse can be served in individual cookie shells known as "tulips". (The recipe for tulips belongs in another cookbook—too long!)

ABOUT THE AUTHORS...

JACK GREENBERG is Dean of Columbia College. From 1984 to 1989, he was Vice Dean and Professor of Law at Columbia Law School. He was Assistant Counsel from 1949 to 1961, and Director Counsel from 1961 to 1984 at the NAACP-Legal Defense and Educational Fund where he argued many leading civil rights cases including the Delaware portion of *Brown v. Board of Education*.

JAMES VORENBERG is Roscoe Pound Professor of Law at Harvard Law School, where he has been Professor of Law since 1962. Between 1981 and 1989 he was Dean of Harvard Law School. He was Law Clerk to Justice Felix Frankfurter from 1953 to 1954 and partner at Ropes & Gray from 1960 to 1962. He was Associate Special Prosecutor of the Watergate Special Prosecution Force from 1973 to 1975.